"As you read *Experiencing God in Your Story*, don't be surprised if you say, 'Wow, this is fresh bread.' Whether it's a story about a peach pie or having God speak to you at 3:00 a.m. in a recliner, Dr. Edwards invites the reader to experience God in real life. And using hymns for prayers is brilliant!"

—Dr. H. Robert Rhoden,
Friend and Author

"An old proverb states that a generous soul prospers, and the one that refreshes others will be refreshed. Keith Edwards is a pastor who refreshes others. The thoughts shared in this devotional book are a generous offering of his soul for the refreshing of yours. *Experiencing God in Your Story* has refreshed my soul."

—Rev. Benjamin Rainey Jr.,
Secretary-Treasurer, Potomac Ministry Network

"Several years ago, Keith Edwards and I traveled to northern India to minister to church planters. As I read through this devotional, I had recollections of the many ways he exemplified grace and kindness in his actions. I saw him interact with others as a person who had experienced God in a deep way. This devotional is very unique because of the practical ways it invites us into a deep reflection of our own lives in light of the Scriptures and in light of Keith's own story, which is beautifully woven throughout. It is encouraging and transforming."

—Dr. Albert Appiah,
Pastor, Renewal Christian Center

"As a pastor of an urban congregation just outside New York City, I am keenly aware of how the busyness of life can make it difficult to cultivate a deeply satisfying spiritual life. Keith Edwards not only invites us to set aside time with God but calls us to experience God in every aspect of our lives. I recommend this inspiring devotional to everyone desiring a closer relationship with God. We will be giving a copy to every person who attends our church. Thanks, Keith, for blessing the kingdom!"

—Rev. James M. Armpriester Jr.,
Lead Pastor, Transformation Life Church

"Leadership is not a title but a journey of experiencing our own story and helping others understand theirs by encountering God in the good, the challenging, the disappointing, and the promising times of life. For over 30 years, Keith Edwards has encouraged many to keep going during the difficult moments, has helped us see on the other side of our personal mountains, and has shown us how to experience Jesus no matter what turns of life we may take. *Experiencing God in Your Story* is more than a book of experimental theory. It is the life story of a man who has lived the words he has written and as a personal friend knows that your life will be impacted and changed. Take heart! God is in your story!"

—Rev. Mark Ivey,
Pastor, Christ Alive Church

"For nearly 20 years I have known Keith Edwards to be a man who walks closely with Jesus. As he does, he invites others along the way to love and learn from our amazing God. Keith is a man who has been deeply shaped by God's grace. Jesus looks good in him. As you read Keith's words, you can know that they have been birthed in the presence of God. They have been tested as he has been tested and reveal themselves to be true to God's Spirit and life-giving Word. You are invited through the words of this devotional to take a long walk with Jesus. Read deeply and richly— and be formed by God's grace."

—Rev. Stefanie Chappell,
National Field Director, Chi Alpha Campus Ministries

"I love this book! It was written by someone who walks with God and who wants others to walk with him as well. The clear explication of God's precious Word, the personal stories, the pastoral reflections, the practical questions, and the intimate prayers make this book an excellent guide for anyone who wants to grow in their walk with Jesus. The best part about the book? God is the hero on every page!"

—Dr. Daniel McNaughton,
Professor of Old Testament and Practical Ministry,
Southeastern University;
Author of *Follow* and *The Spiritual Coaching Toolkit*

"For eight years, I've seen Pastor Keith Edwards live a consistent, godly life, walking out on weekdays what he preaches on Sunday. This has applied to life at the boardroom table as well. He is kind, authentic, and motivating, and he unfailingly acts in the best interests of God and others. A collection of life groups was formed around the early chapters of this book, and I was delighted to see the words of *Experiencing God in Your Story* in action in my own circle of seekers and followers. We were drawn in by Pastor Keith's relevant story and held captive by its connection to the Word. We were pushed to think about heavenly provision through well-crafted questions—many resoundingly deep. I'm thankful for this book. Read it if you are hungry to see the goodness of God in a fresh way."

—Dawn Matson,
Board member, Centerpointe Church

"For 20+ years, Keith's friendship, leadership, and heart for God's kingdom has blessed and enriched a wide circle of grateful people; I am enriched to be in that circle. In these days that tend to guzzle our energy and leave us with little in reserve, Dr. Keith Edwards's well-written devotions take us to a Psalm 23 place of restoration. His insightful writing will feed your soul, reset your perspective, and send you on your way with renewed strength and hope. I encourage you to join the circle!"

—Dr. Paul Drost,
Lead Pastor, Grace of Bel Air A/G;
Past National Director of Church Planting,
Assemblies of God, USA

"Most of us do not approach God's Word in a careful way on a daily basis. So many of us rarely journal our impressions of what we are reading in the Bible. What is there to write if we have cut loose from our moorings? But not Keith Edwards. He approaches the Bible daily in a careful and openhearted way. An evident ongoing dialogue with the Holy Spirit is taking place. Journaling is critical to his very life. Because of the strong roots he has developed personally he has had the opportunity to mentor countless pastors, teachers, and fellow travelers on this amazing journey called servant ministry. Prepare yourself to be comforted, challenged, accompanied, and understood. Prepare yourself to return to a tightly attached relationship with the Vine. Your fruitful branch will be climbing many places and will demonstrate amazing fruitfulness."

—Rev. Rocky Grams,
Missionary and Director of River Plate Bible Institute,
Buenos Aires, Argentina

"In a world besieged with a torrent of pressing demands, Dr. Keith Edwards invites us to realize anew the Father's peace and presence. I invite you to delve into these pages and accept the invitation of this devotional to abide more deeply in the Father's love, grace, and power."

—Dr. David J. Kim,
President, University of Valley Forge

"It has been my great privilege to know my friend Dr. Keith Edwards for over 30 years. He is a gifted and remarkable pastor and leader. This book will take you deep into the amazing character of God. You will be challenged to pursue and grow in your walk with him. Prepare to be inspired!"

—Dr. Tedd Manning,
Pastor, Hope Assembly of God

EXPERIENCING GOD IN YOUR STORY

DR. KEITH G. EDWARDS

LUCIDBOOKS

Experiencing God in Your Story

Published by Lucid Books in Houston, TX
www.lucidbookspublishing.com

ISBN-13: 978-1-63296-503-5
eISBN-13: 978-1-63296-502-8

Special Sales: Most Lucid Books titles are available in special quantity discounts. Custom imprinting or excerpting can also be done to fit special needs. For standard bulk orders, go to www.lucidbooksbulk.com. For specialty press or large orders, contact Lucid Books at books@lucidbookspublishing.com.

TABLE OF CONTENTS

DEDICATION

When I look back over my life, I can say only that I am grateful to have grown up in an environment of love. My mom taught me how to love God no matter what life brings my way. As a single woman with three kids, she depended on God's daily bread, the love of family, and a community of believers. My mom took her final breath on September 23, 2020, only a month before I completed the first draft of this devotional. I can hear her saying, "I'm proud of you, son. I love you." I love you too, Mom, and miss you greatly. I dedicate my first published writing to you.

This devotional is also dedicated to my family. At this time, I find myself saying goodbye to many family and spiritual heroes. Each of them has left a mark on my soul that I still cherish. My extended family was everything to us kids. My aunts and uncles all provided book-worthy stories in my life. They loved me, disciplined me, encouraged me, housed me, and, of course, fed me. There isn't enough thanks in the world to express how grateful I am.

This devotional is 58 years in the making, and I've spent 34 of those years with my incredible wife, Esther. The experiences, disciplines, and encouragements found here are lived out by her every day. She is an incredible friend, leader, and mentor to so many people, and she's my greatest cheerleader.

For many years, Esther has heard me say, "I need to write a book." Her love and encouragement have been my inspiration. Her name may not show up on every page, but her inspiration is certainly present. Esther, you are the love of my life and my best friend. We have four beautiful girls, three sons-in-law, and two grandchildren who love Jesus and provide constant joy and sermon illustrations.

Our girls are now amazing young women who love God and love music (thanks again to their mom). They bring us so much joy. It's not often we are all together anymore, but when we are, we tell stories and laugh as if we are telling the stories for the first time. Now we get to watch each of them soar. As Esther says to them often, "We pray our ceiling is your floor."

Esther and I have two grandchildren now, but if we start talking about Caroline Grace and Carson Lee, this book will be one long run-on sentence. They light up our world, and that's all we need to say.

Pastors often get a bad rap, and some perhaps have earned it, but the ones I know deserve deep appreciation and respect. My response to anyone who complains about ministers is constant: "I'm sorry for your experience, but that doesn't sound like the pastors I know." The pastors I know are caring, passionate for God, and want to make a difference for God's kingdom.

Esther and I have served five churches in different capacities. To each we say, "Thank you for investing in us. We have truly enjoyed the journey with you."

To every mentor, coach, friend, colleague, and staff member, you have added value to my life, and I love you dearly. You have guided me by both speaking truth and living lives worth emulating.

I am blessed with amazing friends who for years have walked with me through some *stuff*. I can't imagine my life without them. You know who you are.

FOREWORD

On the following pages, you will catch a glimpse into the devotional life of a modern-day disciple of Jesus. The author is a man of faith—a humble pastor who listens to the voice of God and loves people well. You will read his reflections on Scripture, God, and the church. You will meet his family, his congregation, and his friends. You will cheer his moments of faith, empathize with his pain, and grieve with him through loss.

On the following pages, you will meet my dad.

One of my dad's favorite sayings is "enjoy the journey." He means it literally. Growing up, he regularly startled my sisters and me awake on Sunday mornings—blasting the Brooklyn Tabernacle Choir and dragging us out of bed into a ridiculous shuffle-dance. He was the star of *our* kid choir shows, the inventor of car karaoke, and an all-too-willing Dairy Queen chauffeur. He always has a song at the tip of his tongue, although the lyrics may be a bit improvised. During one particularly difficult season, my dad gave me a booklet of prayers that he was praying over me. One of those prayers highlighted Nehemiah 8:10 (ESV)—"The joy of the LORD is your strength"—and of course, "Enjoy the journey."

My dad loves telling personal stories. You might think that a Christian devotional book should provide a belief checklist with practical applications to ensure spiritual growth. In that case, you will be disappointed. My dad wrote this devotional to share from his experiences with Jesus and journey with you. I assure you that the stories are all true.

Now that I have introduced you to my amazing dad, I must disclose one caveat: he is not the protagonist in these devotionals. Instead, every time we discussed this book, he proclaimed, "God is the hero in every chapter."

His words remind me that the Christian is never actually the hero of his or her story. God is the main character. He is continually whispering to our hearts, guiding our steps, and intervening miraculously, even when we do not fully recognize his presence. These devotionals will gently nudge you to credit God for his catalytic influence on your story as well.

My dad writes, "The distinguishing marks of a follower of Jesus are favor and the presence of God." Neither of these "distinguishing marks" is self-contrived or dependent on us. Favor is an undeserved grace, and the presence of God is similarly bestowed on us. We cannot control, manipulate, or earn either. We may seek the presence of God and ask for favor, but in the end, it is God who gives as he wills. These divine mercies, these gifts from God, characterize Christians simply because they point back to the ultimate source of our salvation and fruit.

The stories in this book may come from my dad's lived experiences, but God emerges as the protagonist. His favor, presence, and voice shaped the outcome of each. As you read these stories and meditate on these devotions, I encourage you to recognize God as the hero of your story as well. In doing so, you will begin to notice the presence and favor of God saturating your own life and igniting joy for the journey.

—Stephanie (Edwards) Weng
October 2020

But thanks be to God, who in Christ always leads us in triumphal procession, and through us spreads the fragrance of the knowledge of him everywhere. For we are the aroma of Christ to God among those who are being saved and among those who are perishing, to one a fragrance from death to death, to the other a fragrance from life to life. Who is sufficient for these things? For we are not, like so many, peddlers of God's word, but as men of sincerity, as commissioned by God, in the sight of God we speak in Christ.

—2 Cor. 2:14–17 ESV

INTRODUCTION

It is a wonderful privilege to call northern Virginia my home. Living close to Washington, DC, the most influential city in the world, provides opportunities and resources unimaginable to most of the world. There is steady and healthy employment available, one of the highest per household incomes in the country, some of the finest universities, plenty of entertainment and tourist destinations, and the list goes on and on. If you can keep up the pace, you can live the American dream.

Living the American dream can be exhilarating, but it can also leave your spiritual and emotional life depleted. Soon you find yourself running on empty.

I usually pay attention to the gas gauge in my car and fill up when I get below a quarter of a tank. But several years ago, I got so caught up in the busyness of life that I overlooked my gauge's warning signal. When my car sputtered and slowed down to a stop, I was upset at the car and the mechanic I recently paid for repairs. I pulled off to a side street and tried to restart it several times before I realized I was simply out of fuel. The warning signs were all there. The gauge was on empty, and there was a red light on next to the gauge that said "empty." Embarrassed, I called my wife, Esther, and asked her to bring me a can of gas. In front of all my fellow Route 50 travelers, I put enough gas in to get to the closest filling station.

If we are not paying attention to our spiritual lives, we will one day find ourselves as I did in my car—running on empty. Perhaps you are already there. We don't know how it happened. The warning signs were all around us, but we became too preoccupied with other things to respond to life's indicator signs.

The good news is that God wants to respond to our emptiness. He is calling us to pull over. He wants to fill us up with his presence so he can bestow grace, love, joy, peace, rest, healing, and power.

Centerpointe Church dedicated the first 40 days of 2019 to concentrated prayer and spiritual renewal. We created space for God to do a deeper work in us so he could do a greater work through us. Some of us were reminded of who God is and reflected on how God met us in the past with his sustaining love and faithfulness. Others discovered new things about God's character, which caused us to worship him in a more profound way.

This season was also a time for us to take an honest look at our lives and allow the Spirit of God to transform us into the people he desired us to be. We had the opportunity to reflect on each lesson; pray over specific areas; and make practical, life-changing decisions.

Furthermore, we created small groups centered on this devotional. I was part of a small men's group, and Esther and I both participated in another group. In the latter group, I asked a couple who did not attend Centerpointe to host the group at their house, and they agreed. The group was very spiritually diverse, allowing for some very interesting discussions. As the weeks went on, we each took deeper steps of faith. It was a wonderful experience of authentic relationships.

Throughout this devotional, you will have some personal insights into my life, but in no means do I prop myself up as a hero. I had a friend once tell me, "Make sure that you are not the hero of your own story." He was right. All good things come from above. I have made far too many mistakes to be called anyone's hero. My goal in sharing stories is to encourage you to share yours in an authentic way that builds deeper relationships.

I believe that everyone can not only experience God but can also know God and have a personal relationship with him. Yes, the same God who created the ever-expanding universe is available to us. I also believe that your relationship with him can deepen as you connect with him on a regular basis. I do not believe that he is hiding from us or playing some kind of cosmic game with us, trying to see how challenging he can make it for us to find him.

To that end, I offer this devotional book. I want you to discover and develop a relationship with God that is personal and intimate. As you read it, I pray that you will see the different attributes of God that will lead you to want to know him even more.

The devotionals contain personal stories meant to jump-start conversations with others. We all have God-revealing stories, and reading this book is a chance to celebrate them with Jesus and open up opportunities to share them with someone else.

This devotional is divided into three sections. The first section, "The Father of a Jesus-Follower," is written to help you understand how Scripture, along with stories of your life, reveal the character, nature, and work of our Heavenly Father. The second section, "The Community of a Jesus-Follower," will help you understand God's work within the context of a community. The last section, "The Disciplines of a Jesus-Follower," will help you understand what it looks like to be a follower of Jesus.

At the end of each devotional, you will have the opportunity to reflect, pray, and share with others what you are learning.

My prayer for you is that you will have a fresh experience with God and enjoy the abundant life he has for you.

Enjoying the journey,

Pastor Kl

SECTION ONE

THE FATHER OF A
JESUS-FOLLOWER

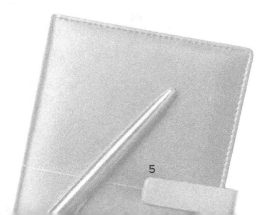

ONE

EXPERIENCE GOD THE FATHER

So you have not received a spirit that makes you fearful slaves. Instead, you received God's Spirit when he adopted you as his own children. Now we call him, "Abba, Father." For his Spirit joins with our spirit to affirm that we are God's children.

—Rom. 8:15–16 NLT

Yet to all who did receive him, to those who believed in his name, he gave the right to become children of God.

—John 1:12–13

One of a believer's favorite images of God is that of a father. It is heard in our prayers, conversations, sermons, and songs. I grew up singing "This Is My Father's World," and at every wedding (including mine and Esther's) we heard "The Lord's Prayer," which, of course, starts with the words "Our Father, which art in heaven." Today we sing "How Deep the Father's Love for Us" and "Good, Good Father." Children's songs include many more. Sadly, the image of God the Father can be so overused that it becomes a cliché and loses its impact on our hearts.

The image of God as a father is also complicated by the different images we conjure up in our heads as a result of our relationship or lack of relationship with our earthly fathers.

If you were to ask me to describe my father, I would be limited to a few facts. I have seen only a few pictures of him, so I know I resemble him physically; but other than that, I couldn't tell you whether he was kind, gentle, cruel, strong, smart, or any other characteristics typically used to describe a father. Throughout my childhood years, I wished I had a dad like all the other boys to play catch with, go fishing with, talk about girls with, buy a car with, and so forth. Although my godly mother made sure I grew up with father figures around me, none of those figures could completely fill the empty place inside. I heard it once said, "Growing up without a dad is like being lost in the woods without a map." I found that to be true as I tried to figure things out on my own.

I could tell you what I believe an ideal father should be like based on my observations of uncles and other men in the church I grew up in, but such observations are limited. I received occasional advice but never had the discipline, intimate conversations, or practical advice I imagined a father would give. As a father myself, I have relied on outside observations, watching closely Esther's relationship with her dad and learning by trial and error.

Thinking of God as a father starts with what we know and experience, but those things are either limiting or distorted. Because humans are not God, even if your dad was nominated for father of the year, he is still a far cry from perfection. If your earthly father was absent or abusive, your view is distorted. When we say God is a good father, we filter the word *good* through our experience.

One day as I was teaching a Sunday school lesson, I came across the passage in Romans that says our spirit cries out "Abba, Father." Somewhere in the notes section of the Bible, I discovered that *abba* is the intimate word for *father*, like the relational word *daddy*.

I had a relationship with God, grew up in the church, and accepted Jesus as my Savior as a child, but after reading the Romans verse, something filled the empty place. I discovered that our Heavenly Father is relational, not just a detached being out in space somewhere. I did not need to feel alone anymore because he was with me. I could not reclaim the past, but I could embrace my new understanding of God as Abba Father.

Calling God our Father is not a new idea only in the New Testament. It is a recurring depiction of the close relationship between the Creator and his people that is commonly seen in the Old Testament.

God is the father of creation.

> *Is this the way you repay the LORD, you foolish and unwise people? Is he not your Father, your Creator, who made you and formed you?*
> —Deut.32:6

Do we not all have one Father? Did not one God create us? Why do we profane the covenant of our ancestors by being unfaithful to one another?
—Mal. 2:10

God is the compassionate father.

As a father has compassion on his children, so the LORD has compassion on those who fear him.
—Ps. 103:13

God is the corrective father.

Because the LORD disciplines those he loves, as a father the son he delights in.
—Prov. 3:12
(This thought is expanded in Hebrews 12:5–11)

God the Father is in the prophetic and poetry writings.

A father to the fatherless, a defender of widows, is God in his holy dwelling.
—Ps. 68:5

He will call out to me, "You are my Father, my God, the Rock my Savior."
—Ps. 89:26

But you are our Father, though Abraham does not know us or Israel acknowledge us; you, LORD, are our Father, our Redeemer from of old is your name.
—Isa. 63:16

Yet you, LORD, you are our Father. We are the clay,
you are the potter; we are all the work of your hand.

—Isa. 64:8

The New Testament writers built upon the thought of having a loving Creator who is willing to call his creation his children. They also emphasize this amazing truth: God is now the *accessible* Father. In the Old Testament, ordinary Israelites could not enter into the presence of God. Only the high priest could enter the most holy part of the tabernacle after a great amount of ceremonial cleansing and strict adherence to many regulations.

When Christ died on the cross, his sacrifice made it possible for all to enter into the very presence of God without the need for a priest. Believers can now approach God as a son or daughter approaches a loving father who loves and cares for his children.

Let us then with confidence draw near to the throne
of grace, that we may receive mercy and find grace to
help in time of need.

—Heb. 4:16 ESV

God's children can bring their cares, worries, frustrations, joys, and laughter before the Father freely and safely.

Being without a dad leaves you always wondering where your place is. I absolutely loved being at my cousins' home to be with my aunts and uncles. They were absolutely the best. But as great as they were, there still remained an awkward truth—I belonged but didn't completely belong. In God's family, I belong as much as anyone. I am at the same table as anyone else, enjoying sonship.

Some people grew up in a religious home where having a relationship with God was based more on rituals, rules, and regulations than relationship. A relationship is different since it is based on receiving God's love rather than earning God's love. It has boundaries like all relationships, but the premise is love.

Moving from religion to relationship is a far leap in some people's hearts, but given time, God will make himself real to each of us, and everything changes. We no longer see him as angry, vindictive, or eager to punish. We see him as a patient Father waiting for us.

When God is our Father, we process life with different questions. We ask, "What brings joy to our Father? How does what I am doing reflect the Father's heart? What is his desire in this situation? What pleases him? How does my life reflect him? Would my Father want this for me?"

We also see our relationships differently. If you and I are both God's children, we are brothers and sisters. As family, I am not looking to step on you to get ahead in life. It also means I look at the opposite gender with dignity and respect rather than with lust.

The older I get, the more I look like my mom and, I assume, my dad. I also look at some of my patterns of behavior and realize that I got them from the environment in which I grew up. Such associations can help open doors. For example, when I was younger, people asked, "Aren't you Ginny's son?" When I said yes, people accepted me because they loved her. The same will happen for you as a child of God. He will open doors you never thought of because you are becoming more like him every day.

As you go through the first part of this devotional, I trust you will experience God as your Father. If you had a great father-child relationship, celebrate it, and express your gratitude often. If you had a less-than-perfect relationship, choose to let God's Word transform your thinking and open your life to God as Father.

TWO

|||||||||||||||||||||||||||||||||||||||||||

EXPERIENCE THE
FATHER'S LOVE

*For this reason I kneel before the Father, from whom
every family in heaven and on earth derives its name.
I pray that out of his glorious riches he may strengthen
you with power through his Spirit in your inner being,
so that Christ may dwell in your hearts through faith.
And I pray that you, being rooted and established in
love, may have power, together with all the Lord's
holy people, to grasp how wide and long and high and
deep is the love of Christ, and to know this love that
surpasses knowledge—that you may be filled to the
measure of all the fullness of God.*

—Eph. 3:14–19

*For I am convinced that neither death nor life, neither
angels nor demons, neither the present nor the future,
nor any powers, neither height nor depth, nor anything
else in all creation, will be able to separate us from the
love of God that is in Christ Jesus our Lord.*

—Rom. 8:38–39

When the Apostle Paul uses the phrase *to grasp* or *to apprehend*, it comes from an old and common verb that means "to lay hold of effectively." It is his prayer that we might grasp God's love through experience, not just intellect.

Paul goes on to say that we are "to know this love that surpasses knowledge." The Greek word for *surpass* literally means "overthrown" and refers to what is thrown over when the container is already full. In other words, Paul is saying, "I want you to know something that is beyond your intellect." All of us know we can feel something without fully comprehending it. A baby feels their mother's love, but what do babies understand about love? They cannot comprehend it, but they can experience it in miraculous ways. In the same way, a child of God does not have to understand all of God's love in order to experience it. As we grow in our relationship with Christ, the mystery of God's love continues to overwhelm us. It is the Father's love for us that transforms us, exciting our hearts and changing our behavior.

Have you ever watched a girl who is engaged? The moment a ring is placed on her finger, she becomes obsessed with preparation. I have watched this close up with my two oldest daughters. Several years ago, Esther and I had the privilege of watching our now son-in-law, Luke get down on his knee and propose to our daughter Brittany. On April 6, 2019, our oldest daughter, Stephanie, along with her now-husband, John, walked through our front door sporting her engagement ring. Both girls were all smiles. Their blue eyes got bluer, and their cheeks got rosier. Their left hands seemed to float in the air. Why? Because someone picked them out of many others to be a bride. They were loved, valued, and significant to the men they also loved and valued.

And then the preparation began.

In his book *When Christ Comes*, Max Lucado writes this:

> Engaged people are obsessed with preparation. The right dress. The right weight. The right hair and the right tux. They want everything to be right. Why? So their fiancée will marry them? No. Just opposite. They want to look their best *because* their fiancée is marrying them.
>
> The same is true for us. We want to look our best for Christ. We want our hearts to be pure and our thoughts to be clean. We want our faces to shine with grace and our eyes to sparkle with love. We want to be prepared. Why? In hopes that he will love us? No. Just the opposite. Because he already does.[1]

Reflection

When did you first experience God's love, and in what ways do you continue to experience it? Let the love of Christ wash over you today like water washing over your hands, cleansing you. Let his love remind you that no matter what, you can never escape his extravagant, unconditional, undeniable, and unfailing love.

---

1. Max Lucado, *When Christ Comes* (Nashville, TN: Thomas Nelson, 1999), 154.

Prayer

God, your love for me goes far beyond my imagination, but I welcome it. Like a child who grabs on to their parent's pant leg and refuses to let go, that's me. I want to live each day with the continuous thoughts of your love.

THREE

‖‖‖‖‖‖‖‖‖‖‖‖‖‖‖‖‖‖‖‖‖‖‖‖‖‖‖‖‖

EXPERIENCE THE FATHER'S GRACE

*For it is by grace you have been saved, through faith—
and this not from yourselves, it is the gift of God— not
by works, so that no one can boast.*

—Eph. 2:8–9

Have you ever apologized for something you really messed up? I don't mean some inconsequential mistake but an intentional act that caused someone pain or suffering? It's humiliating and painful, and the results are unpredictable. Your inner being cries out for forgiveness, but you know it is undeserved. But then the unimaginable happens. Forgiveness is granted. It frees you like nothing you have ever experienced before. This is called grace. There is no way you deserve it, but there it is, relieving you of the weight of guilt and condemnation.

In one of my favorite movies, *Amazing Grace*, there is one scene where John Newton, a repentant slave trader, says to William

Wilberforce, a legislator in the House of Commons, "I remember two things very clearly: I am a great sinner, and Christ is a great Savior."[2] To that I say a big "Amen!"

At the moment of salvation, you did not simply *surrender* your life to Jesus. You also *received* his grace, and although this grace was freely given, it came with a great price. God's grace cost the life of his son Jesus who died on a cross for our sins. You didn't earn it, and you don't deserve it. Grace is an offer of what we do not deserve.

The Greek word for *grace* is the noun *charis,* which refers to an unmerited, favorable disposition toward someone or something. It is commonly used in relation to salvation, especially in Paul's writings, to explain that salvation comes from God's own choice to show favor in redeeming lost persons through faith in Christ.

Andy Stanley says this in his book *The Grace of God:*

> To say that someone *deserves* grace is a contradiction in terms. You can no more deserve grace than you can plan your own surprise party. In the same way that planning voids the idea of surprise, so claiming to *deserve* voids the idea of grace. You can ask for it. You can plead for it. But the minute you think you deserve it, the *it* you think you deserve is no longer grace. *It* is something you have earned. But grace can't be earned.[3]

2. John Newton Quotes, *Goodreads,* https://www.goodreads.com/author/quotes/60149.John_Newton.
3. Andy Stanley, *The Grace of God* (Nashville, TN: Thomas Nelson, 2011), Google Books, xiii.

The only proper response to the gift of God's amazing grace is receiving it through faith. Like a gift at Christmas, it must be received in order for the transaction to be complete. Grace is God's provision, and faith is our part.

It is one thing to receive God's grace; it a whole different ball game when we extend grace to others.

To love is a hard thing, and extending grace is not easy. But hatred is much harder, and bitterness brings even more pain. Yes, unforgiveness builds a protective wall around your mind and soul, but you are unaware that the wall really is a prison that keeps you from experiencing the joy of loving someone.

I went to see a man I hadn't seen in 25 years. He was in hospice care alone—no friends and no family. The most care he had experienced in years came from the hands of the good volunteers at Gilchrist, and that care lasted only three days. For more than 20 years, he had lived on the streets around Baltimore, Maryland, and was moved from homeless shelters to detention centers to prisons to the streets. The only relationship he had was found inside a bottle.

This man deserved no grace. He had deserted his family. He had abused himself with alcohol and his wife with anger. He cared not that he had a daughter and two granddaughters. He left behind him a trail of broken promises and a legacy of curses that were the results of his lifestyle. He had earned his fate—aloneness with no one to claim him as a relative.

What makes this personal is that the pain he had inflicted was directed at people close to me. Some people have earned the right to be angry, but God asks us to do something contrary to our natural response: extend grace.

It is when we forgive that we are most like Christ. It's not easy, but the alternative is a prison. In the end, it is the only way to experience freedom. I heard it said once that unforgiveness is like drinking poison and expecting the other person to die.

As freely as you have received forgiveness, freely extend it to others.

Reflection

Think about the grace of God in your life when you first accepted Christ. What did it mean to you then, and what does it mean to you now?

Now think about those to whom you need to extend grace. Ask God to reveal to you what steps you need to make toward that end.

Prayer

To say that your grace is amazing doesn't come close to capturing my thoughts; however, I know that receiving it is just the beginning of experiencing it fully. The more I extend it, the more I experience how truly amazing it is. So help me today to lay aside my hurts so others may experience your grace.

FOUR

‖‖‖‖‖‖‖‖‖‖‖‖‖‖‖‖‖‖‖‖‖‖‖‖‖‖‖‖‖‖‖

EXPERIENCE THE FATHER'S MERCY

But because of his great love for us, God, who is rich in mercy, made us alive with Christ even when we were dead in transgressions—it is by grace you have been saved.

—Eph. 2:4–5

He has showed you, O mortal, what is good. And what does the LORD require of you? To act justly and to love mercy and to walk humbly with your God.

—Mic. 6:8

As an early driver, I received a few speeding tickets. On one occasion, I received an invitation to a court to explain myself before a judge. There was no getting around the fact that I was guilty. I knew it, and the judge knew it. I admitted my guilt and asked the judge to extend mercy, which he granted. I didn't deserve pardon, but I experienced the judge's mercy, although not before I had a clear understanding of the consequences of continual reckless driving. The judge said, "If I see you back in my courtroom in the next two years, I will take your license away."

Throughout the book of Psalms, we read the phrase "Have mercy on me, O Lord." The psalmists knew they deserved punishment, yet they pleaded for *mercy*, a word that is also translated as "compassion." Another translation could be "unexpected kindness." The good news is that God is rich in mercy, and therefore his wrath does not consume us.

Mercy is closely connected to grace in a sense that both are the foundation of forgiveness. Neither is based on merit, but both are received as gifts from God. Like grace, mercy from God is never deserved and is always generated by his love. Salvation is God's merciful act of withholding his wrath and eternal punishment; in his grace, he also grants us forgiveness and eternal life. Mercy is unique since it is sometimes translated as "compassion" or "pity." Jesus was moved with compassion and showed mercy to the hurting, sick, or downcast.

It is interesting to note that mercy is extended from the larger to the smaller, the rich to the poor, the strong to the weak, and the righteous to the sinner. God, who is completely holy, extends mercy to us as sinners. Mike Treneer writes:

> In the Roman arena, the defeated gladiator was killed by the victor. The loser's only hope was that the emperor, as he watched from his rostrum, would give him the "thumbs up," the sign that he was to be spared as an act of imperial favor. If we picture ourselves as a vanquished gladiator thrown to the ground, with our opponent's sword poised over our neck, and

if we imagine looking up in our despair and seeing against all hope that imperial "thumbs up," we may begin to understand the meaning of this aspect of God's mercy. Those times when we feel most keenly our unworthiness to enter the presence of God are the times when we gain the most insight into this aspect of God's mercy. "O Lord, have mercy (*hanan*) on me; heal me, for I have sinned against you" (Ps. 41:4).[4]

Mercy also has a restorative purpose. It seeks to bring healing. The judge did not extend mercy to me without condition; he offered it to me, expecting me to learn a lesson and change my driving behavior. He saw that I was nervous and took pity on me, and he gave me another chance. In the same way, God takes pity on us and grants us mercy, but he does it so we will choose to live differently.

As we have received mercy from God, let us also extend mercy to others. Micah 6:8 tells us that showing mercy is what pleases God. James 2:13 says, "Because judgment without mercy will be shown to anyone who has not been merciful. Mercy triumphs over judgment." If we do not show mercy toward others, if we don't accept people as God accepts them, it is obvious that we have not accepted the mercy of God.

Reflection

When was the last time you experienced mercy? How did it make you feel, and how did you respond?

Where do you need to extend mercy toward others?

---

4. Mike Treneer, "The Mercy of God," *Discipleship Journal*, 38 (November/December 1986).

Prayer

Lord, I can't help but remember all the moments you extended your mercy to me. I am thankful that your mercy is not simply a one-time act but part of who you are. As I humbly receive your mercy, help me reflect on who you are by offering that same mercy to others.

FIVE

EXPERIENCE THE FATHER'S FAITHFULNESS

*Shout for joy to the L*ORD*, all the earth. Worship the
L*ORD *with gladness; come before him with joyful songs.
Know that the L*ORD *is God. It is he who made us, and
we are his; we are his people, the sheep of his pasture.
Enter his gates with thanksgiving and his courts with
praise; give thanks to him and praise his name. For
the L*ORD *is good and his love endures forever; his
faithfulness continues through all generations.*

—Ps. 100:1–5

*Because of the L*ORD'*s great love we are not consumed,
for his compassions never fail. They are new every
morning; great is your faithfulness.*

—Lam. 3:22–23

Some people add value to everyone around them, and we honor them for such things. Others are known for their generosity, compassion, creativity, care, hope, passion, or love for education, the poor, their country, and so forth. But the character trait I admire most is faithfulness. Such was demonstrated by my grandmother.

I spent the first 12 years of my life living with my mom, my two sisters, my aunt, and my grandmother. The house was a small, two-story, three-bedroom, one-bathroom house in Baltimore County, Maryland. Behind it was a small barn for a few animals and a few acres where my uncle kept a few steers, sometimes pigs, sometimes chickens, and a pony named Bozo. To the side of the house was a one-acre lot for gardening where we grew corn, tomatoes, green beans, and an array of other vegetables. But what made it a place of comfort was Grammaw. She simply loved people and enjoyed every moment when someone stopped by to visit. This old farmhouse was a house of peace for many people.

When I became old enough to drive, I frequently stopped by Grammaw's house on my way to anywhere. I got off of Route 83 on the Belfast exit, took a right on York Road, stopped by Grammaw's house, and then drove past where my grandfather was buried. I did so because I knew what to expect at Grammaw's house: a conversation about the family or the church and, of course, food. Grammaw was 83 when she passed away, and I was asked to speak at her funeral. I had one word to say about her: *faithful.*

My grandmother was faithful to her God, her family, and her church. Her faithfulness meant we could count on her to love and care for us. We could also count on her to share the love of God and speak well of her church. There was something steadfast about her, making her home a safe place.

One of the favored character traits about God in Scriptures is his faithfulness. In Hebrew, the word for *faithful* means "steadfast in affection, allegiance, or firm in adherence to promises or in observance of duty." The psalmists repeatedly return to the truth of God's faithfulness, so much so that it is mentioned 32 times. We will never have to wonder about God's faithfulness. Even more amazing is the fact that even when we are faithless, God remains faithful. The love, grace, and mercy we read about earlier never ceases.

Reflection

Who do you know who embodies the idea of faithfulness?

Take a moment and celebrate God's faithfulness. Give him praise as the psalmists did.

Psalm 40:10 says, "I do not hide your righteousness in my heart; I speak of your faithfulness and your saving help. I do not conceal your love and your faithfulness from the great assembly." Consider who you can share God's faithfulness with.

Prayer

Great Is Thy Faithfulness

Great is thy faithfulness, O God my Father,
There is no shadow of turning with thee.
Thou changest not, thy compassions, they fail not;
As thou hast been, thou forever wilt be.

Great is thy faithfulness!
Great is thy faithfulness!
Morning by morning new mercies I see;

All I have needed thy hand hath provided.
Great is thy faithfulness, Lord, unto me!

Summer and winter and springtime and harvest,
Sun, moon, and stars in their courses above
Join with all nature in manifold witness
To thy great faithfulness, mercy, and love.

Pardon for sin and a peace that endureth,
Thine own dear presence to cheer and to guide,
Strength for today and bright hope for tomorrow,
Blessings all mine, with ten thousand beside![5]

---

5. Thomas O. Chisholm, "Great Is Thy Faithfulness," *Hymnary.org*, https://hymnary.org/text/great_is_thy_faithfulness_o_god_my_fathe.

SIX

EXPERIENCE THE FATHER'S GOODNESS

I remain confident of this: I will see the goodness of the
Lord in the land of the living.

—Ps. 27:13

They celebrate your abundant goodness and joyfully
sing of your righteousness.

—Ps. 145:7

Taste and see that the Lord is good.

—Ps. 34:8

It was on Saturday, November 9, 2021 that my father-in-law, Rodolfo Kolbe, at the age of 84, went to be with Jesus. I had the honor of spending some significant time with him in his last few weeks on earth. He loved God and adored his family. His last days were not easy ones, reminding me that death is not the issue—the dying part is. My father-in-law had heart and kidney failure, and to treat one organ caused stress on the other. Even with oxygen, he found it hard to breathe.

To say that he grew up in poverty would be an understatement. He lived in Germany at the beginning of World War II, and his dad was a prisoner of war held in three different prison camps in three different countries. Since his family was poor and he was the smallest in the family, he became the family beggar. Listening to his story brought tears to my eyes as I thought about how hard it is for some people in the world to simply survive. But his story was filled with gratitude, faithfulness, and trust.

His love for God never wavered in his last days. To him, no matter the pain or suffering, God was good. He said over and over in his thick German accent, "The Lord is so good." That was not simply a throwaway or default comment; sometimes he said it in the middle of his struggle to breathe.

Although it may be difficult to understand God's goodness when we see pain, suffering, and the evil of the world, we can trust that at the end of it all, this one attribute of God will prevail—God is good.

The *Easton's Bible Dictionary* points out that "goodness and justice are the several aspects of one unchangeable, infinitely wise, and sovereign moral perfection. God is not sometimes merciful and sometimes just, but he is eternally, infinitely just and merciful. God is infinitely and unchangeably good (Zeph. 3:17), and his goodness is incomprehensible by the finite mind." [6]

If I hear a negative comment concerning someone I know, I can say, "Hmm, I know that person, and that doesn't sound like

---

6. "Goodness of God," *Easton's Bible Dictionary*, https://ccel.org/ccel/easton/ebd2.html?term=Goodness%20of%20God.

him or her. Surely something is missing here." Because I have a relationship with the accused and a history of their goodness, I have learned to trust them. Before a person passes judgment on someone else, they should take the time to get to know them. This truth also applies to our Heavenly Father. Many people have opinions about him based on the actions of people who claim to be his followers, but not everyone represents Jesus well. As a pastor, I regularly give an invitation to people in church to experience for themselves the goodness of God, to discover who God is.

The psalmist wrote, "Taste and see that the LORD is good" (Ps. 34:8). This means to try and experience. The writer is not asking the readers to simply take his word that God is good but to get to know God and see for themselves.

I'm not a person who likes a variety of food. I'm a meat and potatoes guy. This trait can be a challenge when you pastor in a diverse area such as northern Virginia. My wife is usually my food taster. She knows me enough to say, "You will like it," or "You won't like it." But in the end, if I really want to know if something is good, I have to taste it for myself.

Eerdmans Dictionary of the Bible defines *good* like this:

> The biblical writings testify everywhere to God's goodness, including creation and his faithfulness to his covenant with Israel (Exod. 18:9). However, Joshua reminds the Israelite community that the Lord "will turn and do you harm, and consume you, after having done you good," if they forsake God's ways (Josh. 24:20). The exhortation to be faithful to the covenant and walk in God's ways is common in the prophetic literature (Jer. 6:16; Hos. 3:5). The Psalmist gives thanks to God's name "for it is good"

(Ps. 54:6 [MT 8]), and the Spirit and its fruits are good (Ps. 143:10; Gal. 5:22). The Psalmist also emphasizes that there is no good apart from God (Ps. 16:2), for only God is good (Matt. 19:17).[7]

Reflection

When you think about the goodness of God, what comes to your mind?

How have you seen the goodness of God around you?

Prayer

Lord, you are good, and your mercies endure forever and ever. When I look back over the totality of life, I can see your goodness through your creation and works all around. When I go through difficult seasons, remind me of your goodness so I can put my absolute trust in you.

---

7. "Good," *Eerdmans Dictionary of the Bible*, Google Books.

SEVEN

EXPERIENCE THE FATHER'S HEALING

Jesus went through all the towns and villages, teaching in their synagogues, preaching the good news of the kingdom and healing every disease and sickness.

—Matt. 9:35

On May 5, 1990, Esther and I received very difficult news. Our 10-year-old daughter, Stephanie, was diagnosed with juvenile rheumatoid arthritis, a disease we were told she would have for the rest of her life. From that moment, our lives became filled with specialists and medication. We ended up taking her to the Milton S. Hershey Medical Center in Hershey, Pennsylvania, which specializes in the disease. They patiently prepared Esther and me for a difficult season—and they were not kidding.

We watched our little piano-playing, gymnastics-tumbling, dancing girl quickly decline in energy and stamina. She no longer wanted to ride a bike or play with her younger sisters; it simply wore her out. I can still hear the voice of my second daughter, Brittany, yelling from the room, "I hate arthritis!" When I first heard the song "Do You Want to Build a Snowman?" from the movie *Frozen*, I thought of Brittany and her desire to play with Stephanie who did not want to build a snowman anymore.

Stephanie was treated with heavy doses of methotrexate, the chemotherapy drug at the time. Esther and I gave her an injection every other week, and after some time, she seemed better.

In the spring, we sent our girls to camp. We took a red Little Tikes wagon so someone could pull her around because she was too tired to walk across the grounds.

One evening during a service, the kids went to an altar to pray, but Stephanie stayed in her seat. She absolutely loved Jesus and prayed that God would heal her. Sitting alone, God spoke. He said, "Stephanie, I am going to heal you, but it won't be right away." That's a strange thing to say to a 10-year-old, but God also gave her this verse in the Bible that she could hold on to: "Blessed is the one who perseveres under trial because, having stood the test, that person will receive the crown of life that the Lord has promised to those who love him" (James 1:12). When Esther and I heard this, we were elated. Every day we prayed and watched for her healing to take place, but it did not come quickly.

One year later, at the same campground, God made good on his promise. The minister asked people to come to the altar and pray, and Stephanie made her way to the front. While on her knees, God spoke again. "My daughter, I have healed you." She then became aware that she was kneeling, something she was not previously able to do. Can you imagine her excitement as she told her friends and her parents?

It took some time for Esther and me to believe it because we understood the consequences of coming off her medication. One night as Esther was preparing the night's injection, God spoke to her. "Listen to your daughter. I have done my work." Esther put the needle away, and we trusted God. Sure enough, Stephanie's energy came back, and even the doctors at the medical center confirmed that there was no trace of arthritis in her body. This is a great place for an amen! For years we kept that needle as a testimony of God's healing power.

Stephanie went on to receive her degree in music from Evangel University, with an emphasis on piano performance. She later received a master's degree in piano performance from George Mason University. This may sound like braggadocio, but I'm not just a dad bragging on his daughter. We're a family bragging on God.

Oh, the lessons one learns during these trials! I will share one of them later, but the lesson for today is this: God is still in the healing business. Nearly one-fifth of the Gospels are reports of Jesus's miracles. And Jesus commissioned his disciples to continue his basic ministry, including healing. It should be natural for us to ask God to do the miraculous. We not only have the Word of God, but we also know that Jesus still heals today based on stories we have heard or experienced.

Scripture encourages us to boldly present our requests to God, not out of arrogance but out of a relationship with him where there is no intimidation or judgment. We are just like children who ask parents for what they want without fear.

Not every prayer for healing is as dramatic as Stephanie's, and I do not present a healing guarantee. We cannot answer all the questions that come up when we speak of physical healing, but what we do know is that God still heals. He cares for us and is intimately involved with the details of our lives. We also know that he has power over sickness, and we can approach him confidently.

Reflection

When was a time you asked God to heal you and he did?

In what areas do you need healing right now?

Who do you know who also needs to experience God's healing?

Prayer

For myself: Dear Lord, you are a miracle-working God, and I come boldly into your throne room, not out of arrogance but as your child, confident that you care for me and the concern that is on my heart. Out of your great love and compassion, bring healing to my life. I wait patiently for your healing, and I will trust you in all things.

For others: Dear Lord, _____ needs you today, and I bring them to you, asking you to show yourself as the miracle-working God I know you are. Have mercy on them today. Most of all, remind them of your presence and how much you love them.

EIGHT

EXPERIENCE THE FATHER'S PROVISION

And my God will meet all your needs according to the riches of his glory in Christ Jesus.

—Phil. 4:19

On December 9, 2018, a dear friend of Centerpointe Church left this earth to be with Jesus. He was a man filled with joy, love, and wisdom. I can distinctly remember one conversation I had with him concerning provision after he asked me to pray with him about a financial issue. After I prayed, the Holy Spirit prompted me to declare, "You have too much history with God's provision to think he will let you down now." I have repeated that sentence hundreds of times since then, for it is a statement of thanksgiving and recognition of God's provision.

To say that God is our provider goes far beyond our finances. It is to say that God is our ultimate source for every area of our lives. Although we like to project the impression that we are self-made people, the reality is that no matter how strong, self-secure, or self-sufficient we pretend to be, we are completely dependent on God.

In Scripture, it was Abraham who first identified God as a provider when he was about to sacrifice his son Isaac on an altar. In that moment, an angel intervened and sent a ram, which Abraham sacrificed instead of his son. Afterward, he called the place the Lord Will Provide, or Jehovah-Jireh. This is one of those stories in the Old Testament that looks forward to Jesus as the sacrificial Lamb of God, providing a way for our salvation.

In fall 2017, our church experienced a significant shortfall in funds. Several key givers had moved away, and we did not know how we were going to make up for the loss. I was in the process of drafting a letter to the congregation to let them know about the situation and encourage them to give an end-of-the-year gift.

Our board requested that before we ask the people, we ask God (always a good suggestion). We gathered in the sanctuary, walked around independently for some time, and reconvened at the front of the church. One of our board members said that God wants to encourage us to make wise choices now in order to prepare ourselves for a future when we have greater resources. I thought, "Okay, that's fine, but it doesn't solve our problem now." As we each took turns praying out loud, one of our board members spoke up, and he was visibly nervous. He had not been used in the prophetic gifts before, but he said he had this word from God: "I will supply what you need even before you ask."

We were asking for $50,000, and until then, we had never received a gift that size. We received this board member's prophecy with enthusiasm. The next day, I was the first one at the mailbox, believing God would send a check.

After a few weeks of no financial movement, we drafted the end-of-the-year giving letter, planning to send it on Tuesday afternoon of the following week. That Monday, I received a phone call from someone who wanted to have breakfast the next day. This man had been generous in the past but not at the level of our need. As we sat in Panera Bread, he reached into his pocket and pulled out an envelope. He mentioned that his job wanted some of the employees to cash in some of their stock options, so he did. As he talked, I stared at the envelope. Finally, I got the nerve to ask if I could open it. When I looked at the check, you can guess what I saw. The amount was $50,000, and it had come the morning before I planned to send out the letter. Before I could pull out of the parking lot, I had the board member who had prophesied on the phone. "Guess what! You heard from God!" We celebrated together and were reminded one more time that God is our provider.

When we gain a deeper understanding of his provision in our lives, we also gain a fuller sense of gratitude. We begin to recognize God's provision in small ways as well as obvious ways. We also develop a sense of humility and trust, which keeps us dependent on God's help.

If you are running low on your own resources, remember and repeat this: "We have so much history with God's provision that we have no reason to doubt him now."

Reflection

In what ways does understanding God's provision change you?

What are small ways God has provided for you?

What are large ways God has provided for you?

Take some time to thank God for his provision.

How are you still trusting God to provide for you?

Prayer

'Tis So Sweet to Trust in Jesus

'Tis so sweet to trust in Jesus,
Just to take Him at His Word
Just to rest upon His promise,
Just to know, Thus saith the Lord.

Jesus, Jesus, how I trust Him,
How I've proved Him o'er and o'er,
Jesus, Jesus, precious Jesus!
Oh, for grace to trust Him more.

Oh, how sweet to trust in Jesus,
Just to trust His cleansing blood;
Just in simple faith to plunge me,
'Neath the healing, cleansing flood.

Yes, 'tis sweet to trust in Jesus,
Just from sin and self to cease;
Just from Jesus simply taking
Life, and rest, and joy, and peace.

I'm so glad I learned to trust Thee,
Precious Jesus, Savior, Friend;
And I know that Thou art with me,
Wilt be with me to the end.

NINE

EXPERIENCE THE FATHER'S PEACE

You will keep in perfect peace those whose minds are steadfast, because they trust in you. Trust in the LORD *forever, for the* LORD, *the* LORD *himself, is the Rock eternal.*

—Isa. 26:3–4

Always be full of joy in the Lord. I say it again—rejoice! Let everyone see that you are considerate in all you do. Remember, the Lord is coming soon. Don't worry about anything; instead, pray about everything. Tell God what you need, and thank him for all he has done. Then you will experience God's peace, which exceeds anything we can understand. His peace will guard your hearts and minds as you live in Christ Jesus. And now, dear brothers and sisters, one final thing. Fix your thoughts on what is true, and honorable,

and right, and pure, and lovely, and admirable. Think
about things that are excellent and worthy of praise.
Keep putting into practice all you learned and received
from me—everything you heard from me and saw me
doing. Then the God of peace will be with you.

—Phil. 4:4–9 NLT

The Old Testament word for *peace* is the word *shalom*, which
means "wholeness" or "well-being." It is the harmonious state of
soul and mind, both externally and internally, and is often used as
a greeting or a farewell to express blessing.

To experience peace is a wonderful thing until the storms of
life, which none of us are immune to, show up. I heard once that
we are either going into a storm, currently in a storm, or coming
out of a storm. Either way, there is a storm around us somewhere.
Thankfully, biblical peace is unrelated to our circumstances; it is
a goodness of life that is not measured by what is happening to us
externally.

A brief look at our passage in Isaiah tells us how to experience
peace even in the midst of the storm. The word *steadfast* is also
translated as "stayed, fixed, or residing in." The thought here is to
intentionally take our mind to God's residence. When our mind
is continually residing in a place of God's presence, we may be in
the midst of great trials yet still possess biblical peace.

The Philippians passage helps us understand the process of
experiencing peace. We are to rejoice, remember, pray, and give
thanks. In doing so, we are fixing our thought life on God, his
Word, his works, and his love. Then we can experience his peace,
which surpasses our ability to understand how it all works.

I came to experience the true meaning of Philippians 4 in
1991. For context, refer back to the devotional about Stephanie's

healing. Things changed in our house that year. There were days when I carried her from her bed to the bathroom. The weight of our daughter's sickness was almost more than we could stand. The church was experiencing growth and a spiritual awakening. People were being saved, and some were being healed. In those moments, we prayed that Stephanie would be one of them, but healing did not happen.

The heaviest weight came upon me one day as I stood on the 10th tee, golf club in hand, at the Greencastle, Pennsylvania, golf course. It was one of those days when you just know things are going your way (except maybe your golf game). I was there with three other ministers, the weather was perfect, and the scenery was as picturesque as a postcard. My cell phone rang (to the annoyance of my golfing friends); my wife was on the other end. "It's not good. Stephanie is having a flare, and she can hardly move. She is staying home again." *Flare* is a word that will always have a painful place in our hearts because it was our code word to mean my daughter was in pain. Her type of arthritis was polyarticular rheumatoid arthritis, which means the pain can be in one joint or every joint. The attacks were random. *Flare* meant every joint.

It was in that moment that the weight of my 10-year-old daughter's sickness came crashing in around me. Her suffering was a brutal blow as we realized that she might never grow out of it. I looked at my friends, bowed my head, and began to weep. I told them what was going on with Stephanie and how helpless I felt.

I will never forget the impact of Terry, Brian, and Greg as they gathered around me, put their hands on my shoulders, and without the slightest embarrassment or hesitation, prayed for Stephanie, my family, and me. God's presence overwhelmed me and gave me a new perspective. I then knew that no matter what would happen next, God would receive glory and honor through this storm.

Just as when the friends of the paraplegic man took their friend to Jesus and lowered him with ropes through a roof, my friends took me to Jesus. I had run out of prayers and out of ideas. I was empty and overwhelmed. When my friends took me to Jesus, I was surrounded not only by friends but also by God's peace. I clearly understood what it meant to have peace that passes all understanding. His peace does exceed my comprehension. His peace stands guard around my heart and mind.

Reflection

In what ways have you experienced God's peace?

In what areas do you need to experience God's peace?

Prayer

Lord, my storm is more than I can bear. I know you are with me, but like the disciples, I feel as though you are asleep. I ask you to come to my rescue. Stand up and speak peace to my situation and peace to my heart. I trust you today to guide me through this. In faith I receive your peace.

TEN

|||||||||||||||||||||||||||||||||||||||||||||||||

EXPERIENCE THE FATHER'S WISDOM

Blessed are those who find wisdom, those who gain understanding.

—Prov. 3:13

If any of you lacks wisdom, you should ask God, who gives generously to all without finding fault, and it will be given to you.

—James 1:5

My son, if you accept my words and store up my commands within you, turning your ear to wisdom and applying your heart to understanding—indeed, if you call out for insight and cry aloud for understanding, and if you look for it as for silver and search for it as for hidden treasure, then you will understand the fear of the LORD and find the knowledge of God.

—Prov. 2:1–5

For lack of guidance a nation falls, but victory is won through many advisers.

—Prov. 11:14

The year 2020 was a year to forget—or at least a year we want to forget. But like a horror film, there are some things you can't unsee.

When that year began, "2020 Vision" was the title of thousands of sermons across the country. How could it not be? For Centerpointe Church, the year began with excitement and energy. For four years, we had waited for this moment. We were selling our property and launching into a new season of opportunity. The first week of January, we began meeting in a theater and miraculously found office space in Fairfax Corner, right next to our theater space. We were living the dream—until we weren't. Five weeks into our move, COVID-19 showed up, and in a week, like every church in the world, our service went online. In May, the death of George Floyd caused nationwide riots. If that wasn't enough, we then experienced a world-class crazy presidential race.

We had set sail on a cruise ship full of life, and when we got to the middle of the ocean, the ship sank without lifeboats. We swam north, but there was no land; we swam south, and there was no land. We were doggie-paddling, looking for direction, and it wasn't long before the sharks started circling.

When COVID-19 hit, it seemed that no matter what decision we made, someone was upset. When the racial tensions rose, no matter what we said, someone was upset. And who really knows what to say about the elections?

For 34 years, I have prayed for three things on a consistent basis: wisdom, discernment, and courage. Wisdom goes far beyond information. Wisdom is a matter of how you process information and experiences and then apply them to daily life. Godly wisdom brings a deep-seated understanding that God is in control and will eventually have his way. Discernment understands the different voices that are speaking—the voice inside your head, the voice from outside with ulterior motives, and the enemy's voice that's trying to distract you. Ultimately, we strive to listen to what God is saying in the moment. Finally, courage is the backbone we need to live in obedience to God, no matter what the fallout might be.

The way to wisdom is laid out in Scripture, and the first step—ask—is the simplest. God promises in James 1:5 that if we seek wisdom, he is more than willing to continually give us wisdom *without finding fault.* Those three words are my favorite part of the passage. God is not in heaven eager to remind us how big of a failure we are. Our own minds will take care of that. God doesn't get a kick out of saying, "I told you so." When we ask for wisdom, he gives us a fresh start.

The second step requires effort. Proverbs tells us that we are to accept and store God's Word in our hearts, turn our ear (or pay close attention to), apply our hearts, call and cry out, and look and search for it. These are not passive pursuits, but rather daily disciplines that take effort, time, energy, work, concentration, and focus. We are forced to ask, "What does the Word have to say?" Some things are very clear in Scripture: do not steal, do not commit adultery, do not lie. Other questions require study, prayer, and meditation.

Additionally, wisdom is found in a multitude of counselors. I am blessed to have teachers, friends, mentors, coaches, board members, leadership teams, and family. These people know me and bring their perspectives to me with love and concern.

My most recent weighty decision concerned a close and personal family matter. I honestly had no frame of reference and no sense of direction. I knew that whatever decision I made, it was going to hurt. I decided to call a family member I hadn't talked to in years but had loved and respected my whole life. The conversation was like eating a full and satisfying meal. It didn't make the consequences better, but I was able to make the decision with confidence. I was able to rest, knowing I had made the best decision I could.

Reflection

Think about the last major decision you made. How did you reach that decision? How did you involve God in making the decision? Is there anything you could have done differently?

In what ways do you need God's wisdom in your life now?

What does God's Word have to say about your decision?

What do your closest friends and advisers have to say about your decision?

What do you need to do right now to move forward?

Prayer

Lord, today I will face things I cannot handle on my own. There will be decisions to make, and I desire to honor you in each of them. Give me wisdom to face each one. I am grateful that you do not seek to condemn me for my past poor choices as you are leading me into new and more fruitful ones.

||||||||||||||||||||||||||||||||||||||||||||||

ELEVEN

EXPERIENCE THE FATHER'S STRENGTH

Your arm is endowed with power; your hand is strong, your right hand exalted.

—Ps. 89:13

He tends his flock like a shepherd: He gathers the lambs in his arms and carries them close to his heart; he gently leads those that have young. Who has measured the waters in the hollow of his hand, or with the breadth of his hand marked off the heavens? Who has held the dust of the earth in a basket, or weighed the mountains on the scales and the hills in a balance?

—Isa. 40:11–12

Just leave it in God's hands.

How many times have you heard this advice, and how many times have you offered it to someone else? Something is going wrong, and we are looking for an immediate resolution. We are spending a great emotional price, and nothing is working. We go to someone for some friendly advice, and they say, "Put it in God's hands," and we think to ourselves, "If only it were that easy."

But wait. This advice, although seemingly flippant and dismissive, just might be precisely what is needed, but only if you understand what it truly means and what kind of place God's hand is.

When the Bible speaks of God's hand, it is what we call *anthropomorphism*, the attribution of human characteristics or behavior to God. Although God is not limited like we are in our senses, this language serves a positive purpose of understanding who God is. In this case, he is a God of power and might.

David refers to the *right* hand for a purpose. The right hand was considered the strongest hand because it held the sword while the left hand held the shield. David uses the expression *right hand* 35 times in the book of Psalms to emphasize God's power and strength. To place something in God's hands is to say his strength is now my strength. There is a transference of power that leads to confidence and assurance, which means I can go through times of fear and uncertainty.

Picture a defenseless child holding the strong hand of his or her father. This image shows a little one assuming an extension of the father's power. The connection of the hands is the difference between confidence and fear; it is a safe place where a powerful hand offers transfused inner strength and direction. David reached out the imagined hands of his soul to the outstretched hand of God.

EXPERIENCE THE FATHER'S STRENGTH

As a father of four daughters, I have experienced this image hundreds of times while walking with my girls in a crowd or an unfamiliar place. When one of my girls was really afraid, they practically crawled up my leg to get into my arms where they could bury their face in my chest. Such is the image in Isaiah 40:11 where "He gathers the lambs in his arms and carries them close to his heart."

Knowing that we or our loved ones are in God's hands does not preclude harm befalling us or them, but it does mean we are not alone and that we can find emotional and spiritual strength while trusting him. Now when you hear someone say, "Leave it in God's hands," you can rest assured that in his hands you will find strength that is beyond all you can ask or imagine.

Pastor Erwin McManus tells of a time when he was with a friend of 20 years, talking about the future. His friend had resigned his church and was taking time for restoration and renewal. The friend shared this, which I think is a profound statement that all ministers need to catch: "I don't know the path, so I'm choosing the environment." McManus wrote, "More times than we care to admit, we simply don't know what the next step is. But if our hearts are bound to the heart of God, we are never lost."[8]

Reflection

In what ways have you seen God's power working in your life in difficult seasons?

In what ways do you need to experience God's power right now?

Choose the environment of God's powerful arms. Keep your hands and heart attached to his.

---

8. Erwin McManus, *An Unstoppable Force: Daring to Become the Church God Had in Mind* (Colorado Springs: David C. Cook, 2013), 77.

Prayer
Declare this hymn of the church written by Edward Mote in 1834:

My Hope Is Built

My hope is built on nothing less
than Jesus' blood and righteousness.
I dare not trust the sweetest frame
but wholly lean on Jesus' name

On Christ the solid rock I stand,
all other ground is sinking sand;
all other ground is sinking sand.

When darkness veils his lovely face,
I rest on his unchanging grace.
In every high and stormy gale,
my anchor holds within the veil.

On Christ the solid rock I stand,
all other ground is sinking sand;
all other ground is sinking sand.

His oath, his covenant, his blood
supports me in the whelming flood.
When all around my soul gives way,
he then is all my hope and stay.

On Christ the solid rock I stand,
all other ground is sinking sand;
all other ground is sinking sand.

When He shall come with trumpet sound,
O may I then in him be found!
Dressed in his righteousness alone,
faultless to stand before the throne!

On Christ the solid rock I stand,
all other ground is sinking sand;
all other ground is sinking sand.[9]

---

9. Edward Mote, "My Hope Is Built," Hymnsite.com, https://www.hymnsite.com/lyrics/umh368.sht.

TWELVE

EXPERIENCE THE FATHER'S PRESENCE

Moses said to the Lord *... "If you are pleased with me, teach me your ways so I may know you and continue to find favor with you. Remember that this nation is your people." The* Lord *replied, "My Presence will go with you, and I will give you rest." Then Moses said to him, "If your Presence does not go with us, do not send us up from here. How will anyone know that you are pleased with me and with your people unless you go with us? What else will distinguish me and your people from all the other people on the face of the earth?"*

—Exod. 33:12–16

The distinguishing marks of a follower of Jesus are favor and the presence of God. Neither one is tangible, but both are recognizable and certainly noticeable when they're missing. Both were so crucial to Moses that he didn't want to go anywhere without them. Our passage shows Moses' relentless pleading for God's continual favor and presence. You can feel a sense of powerlessness in Moses' voice; he would rather stay in the desert than be without God.

I often pray the same prayer, especially as it relates to Centerpointe Church. We knew in 2019 that he was leading us to a new location, and we wanted to make sure we didn't take even one step without him. We believed as Moses believed—how would the community know we were different from any other business that relocates? I contend that the presence of God is the only thing that distinguishes the church in a community from any other business. A theater can put on a show and gather a crowd, a hospital can give care, and a school can add knowledge, but only the body of Christ can bring the presence of God to a community.

The phrase *presence of God* is mysterious. It seems strange and unattainable. So what was Moses asking for, and how can we experience this presence?

The presence of God is the constant awareness that God is with us. The primary manifestation of God's presence in the Old Testament was the tabernacle and the Ark of the Covenant, which was used to lead God's people on their journey to Canaan and into battle with bold confidence. Exodus tells us that the Israelites were also led by a pillar of cloud during the day and a pillar of fire at night. "Neither the pillar of cloud by day nor the pillar of fire by night left its place in front of the people" (Exod. 13:22).

Today, as in the New Testament, the primary manifestation of the presence of God is the work of the Holy Spirit living in our lives, guiding, giving wisdom, comforting, convicting, and empowering us. We may not be able to control God's presence, but we can nurture it through the following acts:

- Daily prayer and Scripture reading—setting our minds on God and his ways.
- Worship—feeding our minds with God's goodness. We can read a psalm, an old church hymn, or a chorus. We can listen to Christian music in the car. We can listen to Scripture while we exercise.
- Moments of reflection and refocus throughout the day— brings us back to God and allows him to guide us in our decisions.
- Gratitude—reminding us that all good things come from God.
- Risk—doing something outside your comfort zone allows God to show up and give you boldness.

On A Personal Note: Visiting a family in the hospital is always a humbling experience for any pastor. In this setting, we become very aware of our inadequacy. The words we have to offer often feel shallow and helpless. However, I have learned that explanations and answers are not why people are glad to see a pastor, an elder, or a fellow believer. They want someone who represents the presence of God and the comfort of the Holy Spirit.

Reflection

What are the best ways you have found to nurture the presence of God in your life?

What other ways do you think would be helpful to experience a greater awareness of God's presence in your life?

Prayer

Lord, without your presence in my life, I am lost. I thank you for every moment I recognize your presence with me and also for the moments I was not aware of your presence, though you were there nonetheless.

I invite you to fill my heart with your love and my mind with a deeper understanding of who you are. I invite you into all the decisions I have to make today, and I will give you thanks in all things.

THIRTEEN

EXPERIENCE THE FATHER'S JOY

But let the godly rejoice. Let them be glad in God's presence. Let them be filled with joy.

—Ps. 68:3 NLT

Do not grieve, for the joy of the LORD is your strength.

—Neh. 8:10

The thief comes only to steal and kill and destroy; I have come that they may have life, and have it to the full ["more abundantly" in the King James version].

—John 10:10

Joy is a vital part of the Christian life and one that is too often neglected. I have noticed that too many believers walk around looking as if there is a gray cloud hanging over them, and then they wonder why no one wants to follow them. They remind me of

Eeyore, one of my favorite Winnie the Pooh characters. No matter what goes right in his life, he finds a way to be unhappy. Why would anyone be attracted to Jesus when they see Christians in perpetual sadness?

There are 254 verses about joy in the Bible, which indicates that joy in life is not only possible but also expected for followers of Jesus. This is not just a temporary, fleeting high but something that endures through both good and bad seasons of life.

Nehemiah tells us that the joy of the Lord provides us strength because it gives us the capacity to overcome our trials. James 1:3 teaches us that trials develop perseverance. And perseverance produces character, which leaves a lasting legacy of godliness. Jesus-followers can expect to experience joy even in the midst of difficulty. Galatians 5 includes joy as one of the fruits of the spirit, along with love, peace, patience, kindness, gentleness, and self-control. None of these stands alone; they are each part of the life of a follower of Jesus.

However, the secret to finding joy is not in the search for joy. I knew a man who believed that the missing ingredient of his life was joy, so he went around searching for it. His mind was consumed by this illusive fruit. He frequently changed churches, joined Bible studies and prayer groups, and looked for a feeling, only to be disappointed again and again. Joy doesn't come to us when we chase it like a dog chasing its tail; rather, it is a byproduct of a relationship with Christ.

As challenging as it may be, we have to shift our attention from difficult circumstances to the person of Christ. The writer of Hebrews tells us that we must fix our eyes on Jesus. "For the joy set before him he endured the cross, scorning its shame" (Heb. 12:2). We are to "consider him who endured such opposition from sinners, so that you will not grow weary and lose heart (Heb. 12:3).

59

The joy set before Jesus was the hope of a restored relationship with God and man.

One way I have found to shift my attention from trials is to borrow joy from someone else. Often, instead of celebrating with others, we find ourselves feeling jealous, and jealousy leads to resentment and a loss of joy. Instead of complaining about our situation, we can rejoice that someone else is experiencing victory. Is anyone around you prospering in some way? Rejoice with them. Is anyone around you experiencing a victory? Celebrate with them. In this way, you are taking your eyes off yourself and joining in another's blessing.

Reflection

When was the last time you experienced joy in the midst of a trial? How was it possible?

Who around you is prospering or experiencing a victory? Celebrate God's provision in their life.

Prayer

Lord, I thank you for the joy of the Lord, for it is my strength. I want to be constantly aware of your goodness and grace in my life. May I be a person of joy and encouragement to others.

FOURTEEN

‖‖‖‖‖‖‖‖‖‖‖‖‖‖‖‖‖‖‖‖‖‖‖‖‖‖‖‖‖‖‖‖‖

EXPERIENCE THE FATHER'S BLESSINGS

If you fully obey the Lord *your God and carefully follow all his commands I give you today, the* Lord *your God will set you high above all the nations on earth. All these blessings will come on you and accompany you if you obey the* Lord *your God:*

> *You will be blessed in the city and blessed in the country.*

> *The fruit of your womb will be blessed, and the crops of your land and the young of your livestock—the calves of your herds and the lambs of your flocks.*

> *Your basket and your kneading trough will be blessed.*

You will be blessed when you come in and blessed when you go out.

The LORD will grant that the enemies who rise up against you will be defeated before you. They will come at you from one direction but flee from you in seven.

The LORD will send a blessing on your barns and on everything you put your hand to. The LORD your God will bless you in the land he is giving you.

The LORD will establish you as his holy people, as he promised you on oath, if you keep the commands of the LORD your God and walk in obedience to him. Then all the peoples on earth will see that you are called by the name of the LORD, and they will fear you. The LORD will grant you abundant prosperity—in the fruit of your womb, the young of your livestock and the crops of your ground—in the land he swore to your ancestors to give you.

The LORD will open the heavens, the storehouse of his bounty, to send rain on your land in season and to bless all the work of your hands. You will lend to many nations but will borrow from none. The LORD will make you the head, not the tail. If you pay attention to the commands of the LORD your God that I give you this day and carefully follow them, you will always be at the top, never at the bottom.

Do not turn aside from any of the commands I give you today, to the right or to the left, following other gods and serving them.

—Deut. 28:1–14

Wow! I want to live in this kind of blessing, and I want my children and grandchildren to experience the same. Furthermore, I desire our church to experience the blessings of God. The good news for us is that God is a God waiting to pour out his benefits on his people.

To be faithful to the text, we have to understand that this passage was written to a nation, not just an individual; however, the basic principles of obedience and blessing apply to all of us. The nation of Israel demonstrated over and over again the truth of the passage. When they were faithful to God, they experienced God's blessing in a tangible way. When they were not faithful, they experienced God's discipline.

The Old Testament's word for *blessing* generally denotes a bestowal of good. To live under God's blessing means to live in a condition or state of being in God's grace or favor. God is portrayed as the God of blessing for his people who is waiting to pour out his benefits upon his people. This passage demonstrates the benevolent desire of God to bless his people as a good father desires to bless his children.

There is something powerful and wonderful about a parent's, especially a father's, blessing. I have been to many (when I say *many*, I mean MANY) music recitals and competitions. When the awards were given out, my daughters looked through the crowd to make eye contact with me or Esther for approval. All kids after any performance do the same. More than the blue ribbon at a science fair, more than a trophy or plaque, a child longs for

63

their mom and dad's "great job!" If blessing has anything to do with approval, children long for their father's blessing and will do almost anything to get it. I certainly know the feeling.

Growing up without a dad, I longed for male role models in my life to affirm me. Fortunately for me, my mom made sure I was surrounded by uncles and men at church who filled that gap as much as they could. When there was a sense of blessing, my outlook on life was different. I walked with more confidence and was able to power through obstacles.

What is true in the natural is also true in the spiritual. We long to hear the words *well done* by a Heavenly Father. We want to know we please him and are living in his favor and blessing. The good news is that it is God's nature to want to bless us. The God of the Bible does not wish to withhold from us; in fact, he takes joy in blessing us. The more we get to know him, the more we see someone who passionately loves us.

God's requirements for blessing are found in some of the words in Deuteronomy 28:1—"fully obey" and "carefully follow." At first glance, these requirements sound similar to other religions, but there is a difference, much like a healthy home versus a dysfunctional home. In a healthy home, children don't try to make the parents want them by their obedience; they know they are loved. However, when a child does live in obedience, parents are even more apt to be generous.

If we want to experience the blessings of God, we must follow him with all our heart, soul, mind, and strength. This is not a case for works-based theology; it is merely a statement of relational surrender.

Reflection

In what ways have you experienced God's blessing?

What does "relational surrender" mean?

How is obedience linked to blessing?

For further study, read all of Deuteronomy 28. What insight can we gain concerning obedience and blessing?

Prayer

Lord, give me a different perspective on blessing. Help me grasp how much you love to bless me, and help me recognize your blessings in the smallest ways as well as the more obvious ones.

FIFTEEN

EXPERIENCE THE FATHER'S FAVOR

May the favor of the Lord our God rest on us; establish the work of our hands for us—yes, establish the work of our hands.

—Ps. 90:17

My son, do not forget my teaching, but keep my commands in your heart, for they will prolong your life many years and bring you peace and prosperity. Let love and faithfulness never leave you; bind them around your neck, write them on the tablet of your heart. Then you will win favor and a good name in the sight of God and man.

—Prov. 3:1–4

In July 2014, Esther and I drove our daughter Kristi to Cleveland, Tennessee, to visit Lee University. Walking around campus, I noticed that every building had an engraved stone with the same Scripture reference: Psalm 90:17. We later discovered a bronze statue of a man sitting on a bench with his Bible open to the same verse. My curiosity led me to a verse I have quoted now hundreds of times in prayer. This verse portrays a desperate soul who recognizes his temporary presence in this world and wants to leave a meaningful legacy.

It is often said that favor is when people like you, and you don't know why. This definition is true to some extent. Favor unlocks doors that you thought were closed and brings opportunities you would not have expected. Favor comes from someone with authority or influence giving it to someone with less authority or influence. The person in a higher position holds the key to something desired and hands that key to someone who hadn't earned it yet.

For example, for three years, I worked for Dr. Bob Rhoden, someone I considered one of the greatest leaders in our network. His influence was and still is profound. When he speaks, people take notes. During a funeral I attended, he was the last of seven speakers. As each person spoke, the congregation and I nodded in agreement, but when Dr. Rhoden spoke, I along with others got out our phones to take notes. We knew he was going to drop a wisdom gem, and we did not want to miss it. When I began working with him, I had a few connections and relationships, but after I worked for him, my relationships expanded exponentially. Pastors returned my phone calls, not because of me but because of the favor granted me by Dr. Rhoden. I have learned that favor is a gift placed upon us.

If favor is a gift, I wonder if there is a way to position ourselves to earn it more often. What part do we have in receiving favor? Like a blessing, I believe we can put ourselves in a position of favor. Isaiah 66:2 says, "These are the ones I look on with favor: those who are humble and contrite in spirit, and who tremble at my word."

Humble, contrite, and *tremble at my word* are terms of deep respect. They are also terms of positioning. The *Holman Illustrated Bible Dictionary* says this:

> "Fear" and "love" are both terms found in ancient Near Eastern literature associated with covenant loyalty. To fear God is to have allegiance to Him and consequently to His instructions, thus affecting one's values, convictions, and behavior (Gen. 20:11; Lev. 25:17, 36, 43; 1 Sam. 12:14, 24; Ps. 128:1; Prov. 8:13). True believers are often referred to as those who fear God (Gen. 22:12; Job 1:9; Pss. 31:19; 33:18; 103:11,13,17; 115:11,13; 118:4; Mal. 3:16; 4:2; Luke 1:50). So the fear of God expressed in humble submission and worship is essential to true wisdom (Prov. 9:10; 15:33; Isa. 33:6). A true believer may be defined as one who trembles at God's word (Gen. 22:12; Exod. 1:17; Ps. 119:161; Isa. 66:2, 5; Jer. 23:9).[10]

Proverbs 3:3–4 helps us even more: "Let love and faithfulness never leave you. . . . Then you will win favor and a good name in

---

10. "Fear," *Holman Illustrated Bible Dictionary,* Chad Brand, Eric Mitchell, and Holman Reference Editorial Staff, eds., 2015, Google Books, 561.

the sight of God and man." Be constant. Be consistent. Be in awe of God's Word. Then you will stand under the umbrella of favor.

As my late uncle Harris said to me many times about fishing, "Luck favors a prepared mind."

Reflection

In what ways have you experienced God's favor?

How do you know what God's favor looks like?

In what areas do you need God's favor?

In what ways can you position yourself for favor?

Prayer

Lord, whatever I do, let it be for your honor and glory because that is the only way it will mean anything for future generations. I humbly submit myself to your authority, and I receive from you the gifts of favor and blessing.

||||||||||||||||||||||||||||||||||||||||||||

SIXTEEN

EXPERIENCE THE FATHER'S VOICE, PART 1

The boy Samuel ministered before the LORD under Eli. In those days the word of the LORD was rare; there were not many visions. One night Eli, whose eyes were becoming so weak that he could barely see, was lying down in his usual place. The lamp of God had not yet gone out, and Samuel was lying down in the house of the LORD, where the ark of God was. Then the LORD called Samuel.

Samuel answered, "Here I am." And he ran to Eli and said, "Here I am; you called me."

But Eli said, "I did not call; go back and lie down." So he went and lay down.

Again the LORD called, "Samuel!" And Samuel got up and went to Eli and said, "Here I am; you called me."

"My son," Eli said, "I did not call; go back and lie down."

Now Samuel did not yet know the LORD: The word of the LORD had not yet been revealed to him. A third time the LORD called, "Samuel!" And Samuel got up and went to Eli and said, "Here I am; you called me."

Then Eli realized that the LORD was calling the boy. So Eli told Samuel, "Go and lie down, and if he calls you, say, 'Speak, LORD , for your servant is listening.'" So Samuel went and lay down in his place.

The LORD came and stood there, calling as at the other times, "Samuel! Samuel!"

Then Samuel said, "Speak, for your servant is listening."
—1 Sam. 3:1–10

One Saturday afternoon, a lady in our church made a peach pie. As she was baking, the Lord said to her, "I want you to bake two pies," but she had no idea why. It made no sense to her, but she obeyed the prompting of the Holy Spirit and made a second one. In that Sunday's message, I happened to mention my love for peach pie. When the lady heard this, she also heard the Spirit say to her, "That is why I had you make the second pie. I want you to give it to the pastor as a way of letting him know I love him." She immediately left the church. Although I noticed her leaving,

I didn't give it much thought. By the end of the service, she had returned with a freshly baked peach pie and gave it to me as I was leaving. It sounds shallow, but she was thrilled to know that she had heard the voice of God, even though it was a strange request. She was thankful that she was obedient to the voice and even more excited that she could express love to her pastor in a tangible way. And I was also thrilled because I got an amazing peach pie to share with my family.

Stories like this remind us that God still speaks to us if we will take time to listen. During the COVID-19 crisis of 2020, I took a long walk in Virginia Beach to pray. I was concerned about the missionaries we support on a monthly basis and was wondering how their ministries and finances were holding up. I can't say that I saw God's handwriting in the sky, but I felt a nudge to ask the church board to double our support for two months and ask the people to consider doing the same. I called the missions director of our network to run the idea by him. He told me that he had just called one of the national directors of missions for the Assemblies of God, and they talked about that exact thing and, even more, that exact amount. This conversation confirmed to both of us that God was speaking.

Sometimes what we hear from God is seemingly insignificant, and other times God speaks to us in ways that impact the lives of many.

By emphasizing the last sentence in our study passage, we see the process of how Samuel heard God's voice and gave us a pattern to follow.

Speak – Samuel sought God's voice.

Your servant – Samuel positioned himself as a servant.

Is listening – This is called "active listening" with a commitment to obey.

If you continue to read the chapter, you will see that God asked Samuel to pronounce judgment on his mentor's disobedient sons. Reluctantly, Samuel obeyed. God eventually elevated Samuel as Israel's primary prophet and leader. Here is a tip for you: if you are going to speak judgment on someone in authority, you'd better know it is God's voice you are hearing.

The prayer of Samuel served him well his whole life and is the same prayer we ought to pray as we follow Jesus.

Reflection

When did you hear God speak to you and ask you to do something that seemed insignificant? How did you respond? What was the result?

When did you or someone you know listen to God's voice and make a profound difference in the lives of others?

What is God saying to you today?

Prayer

Take a moment to repeat Samuel's prayer several times, emphasizing each word. Let this prayer be a commitment to serve and obey God's voice.

Speak
Your servant
Is listening

SEVENTEEN

EXPERIENCE THE FATHER'S VOICE, PART 2 (YES, THERE IS MORE)

Then a great and powerful wind tore the mountains apart and shattered the rocks before the LORD, but the LORD was not in the wind. After the wind there was an earthquake, but the LORD was not in the earthquake. After the earthquake came a fire, but the LORD was not in the fire. And after the fire came a gentle whisper.

—1 Kings 19:11–12

Every once in a while, it would be nice to hear God speak from a burning bush or in some other dramatic fashion as he did in the Old Testament. God spoke through earthquakes, fire, angels, prophets, and visible writing on a wall. But why doesn't he just step up to the mic, turn up the volume, and drown out the competition? It seems as though we want the dramatic, but he often gives us a whisper.

In the New Testament, God spoke in a dramatic fashion only a few times, and most of those times, the purpose was to affirm Jesus's divinity, such as when he was baptized. The Spirit of God descended like a dove, and a voice from heaven said, "This is my Son, whom I love; with him I am well pleased" (Matt. 3:17). That kind of thing still happens today, especially to those who live in a Muslim majority country and who have seen Jesus in a vision or dream. Although these accounts are incredible, we are still left with this question: How can we hear God's voice in our life on a regular basis? We know he is not silent, but it often feels that way. Maybe, just maybe, it is because when we pray, we do so with our own agenda.

In her book *Strengthening the Soul of Your Leadership*, Ruth Haley Barton discusses the process of discerning God's will and the need to pray for indifference. Here's what she wrote:

> We need to also pray for *indifference*. This is not the kind of indifference that we associate with apathy; rather, it is the prayer that we would be indifferent to everything but the will of God. Indifference in the discernment process means that I am indifferent to matters of ego, prestige, organizational politics, personal advantage, personal comfort or favor, or even my own pet project. As Danny Morris and Charles Olsen put it: "God's will, nothing more, nothing less, nothing else."[11]

In 2013, on a mission's trip to Argentina, I had a chance to have coffee with the director of the Bible college we were helping.

---

11. Ruth Haley Barton, *Strengthening the Soul of Your Leadership: Seeking God in the Crucible of Ministry* (Downers Grove, IL: InterVarsity Press, 2008), 201–202.

During that conversation, I felt God speaking to me about giving part of our church's building fund money to the school. At first, I thought it was just my own internal voice, so I waited and prayed. When I got home, I ran it by Esther, and we prayed together. I processed the idea with our board, and we also prayed. Because this money was designated for another purpose, we needed the approval of the entire Centerpointe membership. In our meeting, we could sense God was directing.

What we did not tell the membership—because it would seem manipulative—was the work God did in Esther's heart to confirm the gift. Esther is very sensitive to the voice of God, but she was struggling with this one until she received a phone call from a friend who was awakened by the Lord to pray for Esther. She felt the Lord was telling her to call Esther because she was wrestling with something that had to do with giving a large amount to missions, but God wanted to let her know that it was in his plan and that he would be honored in the gift.

After the membership voted to give, Esther shared her story, and the church rejoiced together. The following day, our mission's coordinator called the missionary, and we wrote the check. That year we saw 2 Corinthians 9 upfront and personal:

> *The point is this: whoever sows sparingly will also reap sparingly, and whoever sows bountifully will also reap bountifully. Each one must give as he has decided in his heart, not reluctantly or under compulsion, for God loves a cheerful giver. And God is able to make all grace abound to you, so that having all sufficiency in all things at all times, you may abound in every good work.*
>
> —2 Cor. 9:6–8 ESV

In the missions-giving example, we can see these filters for us to discern whether or not we are hearing from God:

1. Do you have a sense that the Spirit put a decision on your heart? Ask God for wisdom and discernment.
2. Is it in line with Scripture? God will never go against his Word!
3. Does it lead you and others into a closer walk with Jesus?
4. Is there confirmation from trusted, godly people?
5. Do you have a sense of peace? God also speaks to us in the negative by withholding his peace.

Reflection

Name a time when you clearly heard God asking you to do something, but you questioned whether or not it was God speaking. How did you come to the conclusion that it was God?

Along with the filters listed above, what are other ways we can know if God is speaking to us?

The Holy Spirit doesn't always ask us to do the dramatic. Often, he speaks to us in our daily routines. How does he do that?

Prayer

Father, right now I lay down my own agenda, and I listen to yours. Help me discern the difference between the voices of the world, the voice of my own selfishness, and the voice of the Holy Spirit. Furthermore, give me the courage to obey what you are saying to me.

EIGHTEEN

EXPERIENCE THE
FATHER'S KINGDOM

And why do you worry about clothes? See how the flowers of the field grow. They do not labor or spin. Yet I tell you that not even Solomon in all his splendor was dressed like one of these. If that is how God clothes the grass of the field, which is here today and tomorrow is thrown into the fire, will he not much more clothe you— you of little faith? So do not worry, saying, "What shall we eat?" or "What shall we drink?" or "What shall we wear?" For the pagans run after all these things, and your heavenly Father knows that you need them. But seek first his kingdom and his righteousness, and all these things will be given to you as well. *Therefore do not worry about tomorrow, for tomorrow will worry about itself. Each day has enough trouble of its own* (emphasis added).

—Matt. 6:28–34

One significant meaning of *seeking* is "to beat the covers for birds." It is a description of a sportsman's method. On Saturdays during the fall, my uncles often took my cousins and me hunting. We took the dogs to a cornfield and walked near the hedges while the dogs went in and tried to scare out a few rabbits. There were many occasions when my uncles sent us boys into the thickets. With sticks in hand, we beat the bushes, and oh, the joy when we saw the bushes rustle and a fluffy cottontail dart out, throwing the dogs barking and my uncles shooting. We had only one thing on our mind: get rabbits. And we were prepared to wade through swamps, climb stumps, push through brier, watch, wait, wriggle, and do everything but fail. We were focused and persistent.

Jesus made the kingdom of God a central theme in his preaching; therefore, it must become our central focus. God's kingdom is not a geographical area such as the Holy Land or the temple. In fact, it is independent of geographical and political entities. The kingdom of God is the rule and reign of God in our hearts and lives. When we are part of the kingdom of God, we have a different perspective on life. We see things differently. In other words, we are not the center of our own universe—Jesus is.

The context of our verses gives meaning. The entire chapter contrasts what it means to seek the kingdom of God versus what we think it takes to satisfy us. It is our natural tendency to want something other than what we already have—new phone, new car, new relationship, new computer, new career, new investment, new workout routine, new clothes, new degree, new plaque on the wall, new tattoo, and the list goes on and on. Christians are not immune to these. We seek a new preacher, new church, new teaching, new Bible study, new spiritual discipline, new song, new worship leader, and new experience. We have become consumers of Christian goods rather than worshipers of God. The chasing never ends and never satisfies.

It is time to stop and say, "He's all I need," because one day he is all you will have.

There is something else concerning the act of seeking. To seek *first* indicates not good and bad or right and wrong, but rather a first and second. God does not forbid us from things we enjoy, but the things we enjoy should rank in their proper place. The kingdom of God is not in opposition to the possessions of this world; it is placed above them. It is higher than the physical and the material. It has to do with the essential purpose of mankind—a life that is more than simple existence.

Seeking the kingdom of God is the antidote to worry. This kingdom is led by the King of kings: King Jesus. And this king is a benevolent, loving, trustworthy, and righteous king. This passage also teaches us that if God provides for the birds and clothes the flowers with beauty, he will care so much more for us. We make a choice to put the kingdom of God first at the moment of conversion, and it is also a choice we make on a daily basis. The results are righteousness, peace, and joy in the Holy Spirit (Rom. 14:17).

Reflection

What does it look like for you to seek first the kingdom of God and his righteousness?

Review the last seven days. How did the kingdom of God rate on your priority list? What can you change about the next seven days?

Prayer

Lord, I confess that most days are consumed with what I want, what I need, and what I care about. I pray that you would shift my thinking to invite your Holy Spirit to lead me in all things so your kingdom is my first priority.

II

EXPERIENCE THE FATHER'S OFFER OF A NEW LIFE

For God so loved the world that he gave his one and only Son, that whoever believes in him shall not perish but have eternal life.

—John 3:16

I have come that they may have life, and have it to the full.

—John 10:10

Jesus performed many other signs in the presence of his disciples, which are not recorded in this book. But these are written that you may believe that Jesus is the Messiah, the Son of God, and that by believing you may have life in his name.

—John 20:30–31

All over the world people are running after things that do not satisfy their hungry souls, leaving a sense of something missing. They want to make a difference, and they want deep relationships, but they remain disconnected. They are fixated on gaining power, building wealth, having a career, and growing a family. These things can be wonderful, but they are never completely satisfying. Only Jesus gives us new life that fills the missing place.

Jesus completes us like nothing else does.

When we moved to Centerpointe Church, the first person who received Christ and was baptized in water was a young man from Iran. If word got out to his home country that he was now a follower of Jesus, his family would be in danger, so he told his brother about a friend he met and was hanging out with. When his brother visited America, he was anxious to meet this new friend—and he did when he came to church. He also surrendered his life to Jesus, and both of their lives were forever changed. Even after they moved away, they often came back on Easter to celebrate their new life in Christ.

The word *life* in Scriptures is translated from the Greek word *zoe*, which means "vitality." Something comes alive in us when we realize our Creator actually loves us, wants to have a relationship with us, and has a plan for our lives. We are born again, which means we are not simply forgiven of sin but completely made new.

This new life is more than just a fresh start; it is a complete rewrite. Jesus doesn't just change a few things in our lives to simply make us better; he transforms us. As the Apostle Paul put it, "If anyone is in Christ, he is a new creation. The old has passed away; behold, the new has come" (2 Cor. 5:17 ESV).

The transformation begins with our relationship with God through Jesus. We acknowledge we are sinners in need of a Savior, and we receive the gift of grace because of what Jesus did on the cross. Because of that, we become children of God. Like a parent reconciled with a child, we are reconciled with God.

The transformation that began in our hearts now finds its way through our whole being. That *zoe* changes my attitude, my behavior, my relationships, and my destination.

In West Virginia, a man in our church was a contractor, known by his employees and family as someone who was always angry. One day, he accepted an invitation by his brother to attend church. It was 40 days before the year 2000—40 days until the year ended, the decade ended, the century ended. I simply asked this question, "How do you want to finish?" I can't say the message was a profound one, but it was profound to him. He and his wife responded to the invitation to make Jesus the Lord of their lives, and the change in his life was dramatic. His anger changed to joy, so much so that his employees took notice. He stopped cursing and started smiling. He found a life worth living. He had new purpose, new joy, new meaning, new patterns of thinking, new relationships, new hopes, and new dreams.

This life is also eternal. Life does not end when we breathe our last breath. The promise we have in Christ is the hope of spending eternity with him.

On Sunday, September 20, 2020, one of the last things my mom said to me was this: "Tomorrow, I'll be in heaven." There was no fear in her eyes, no wondering about her future. Her eternity was secure. Two days later, she arrived at the place she longed for. But Mom's eternity with Christ did not begin when she died; it began when she was a little girl who gave her life to Christ.

Reflection

What is different about your life since you surrendered it to Jesus? Take time to celebrate those changes, and reflect on what life would be like today if you had not changed.

In what ways is God still changing you?

Prayer

Jesus, thank you for this new life I found in you. Thank you for reminding me of my reconciled life in you. Continue to work in me, and change me completely. I want to live my life in such a way that everyone who knew me before becoming your follower will recognize the difference and also want to follow you.

TWENTY

EXPERIENCE THE FATHER'S SON

*But these are written that you may believe that Jesus is
the Messiah, the Son of God, and that by believing you
may have life in his name.*

—John 20:31

I love nativity scenes. They come in all shapes and sizes, depicting
the birth of Jesus Christ in Bethlehem. When Esther and I traveled
to Israel, we noticed that manger scenes were the number-one-
selling item to tourists, especially those made from an olive tree.
Some of them were quite simple, and others were elaborate pieces
of art.

We have always had a nativity scene in our home. One year, I
made a wooden manger, and we put little ceramic figures in and
around it. Stephanie and Brittany were putting it up one year and ar-
guing about how close Mary, the mother of Jesus, was to be to the crib.
So much for peace on earth and good will to all men—or siblings.

Years later, we bought a new nativity set. Frankly, the last one was too white. We had talked about it for a couple of years and finally decided that we needed one in which baby Jesus was not a blond-haired, blue-eyed baby. The irony is that when we took the new one out of the box, Mary was blonde (but I digress). We got one big enough to see but small enough to fit on our upright piano.

Nativity scenes are reminders to us to stop and think about what really happened over 2,000 years ago in a little town of Bethlehem. Jesus, God's Son, our Savior, was born. The problem for so many people is that Jesus is just a ceramic baby figurine. We have seen it so much that it has lost its impact or relevance. Ceramic Jesus comes out on special occasions. He is in paintings, in history books, in church plays, in videos, in stained glass, on coffee mugs, on bracelets, and is even portrayed as a bobble head. He is a nice thought, but he makes no difference.

To many, the manger scene is like a one-act play. The curtain opens, the actors act, Jesus makes an appearance, the audience claps, and the curtain closes. They do not know that the Christmas season is a clarion call to rejoice anew not only with the memory of the babe in the manger but with the constant presence of the risen Savior.

The story we tell has deep meaning. It is the story of God sending his Son into the world to dwell among us to reveal who the Father is. The first chapter of John brings some understanding to that: "So the Word became human and made his home among us. He was full of unfailing love and faithfulness. And we have seen his glory, the glory of the Father's one and only Son. No one has ever seen God. But the unique One, who is himself God, is near to the Father's heart. He has revealed God to us" (John 1:14, 18 NLT).

The Father has been revealed. He has gone beyond parchment and paper. He has gone beyond videos and live drama. He has actually come and pitched his tent in our backyard and beckoned us to watch him and get to know him in the person of his Son, Jesus. When you watch Jesus in action, you watch God in action. When you hear Jesus teach, you hear God teach. When you come to know what Jesus is like, you know what God is like.

I love what Paul wrote in 1 Timothy 1:15: "Here is a trustworthy saying that deserves full acceptance: Christ Jesus came into the world to save sinners—of whom I am the worst." He did not come for trees or bright color packages or lights or presents or school presentations. The gift of God is all about a relationship with us.

The Scriptures were not written to simply inform us or entertain us. They were written to stir our hearts to *believe*. They were not written so we could admire Jesus; they were written so we could follow him. And there is that one word we have to grapple with: *believe*. To believe is to acknowledge the truth as truth. To believe in Jesus is to say that Jesus is who he said he is—the Son of God.

Believing leads to trust. To trust is to rely on and derive confidence in something or someone. We are invited to believe in Jesus Christ the person, not merely his message, his teaching, his example, or his challenge to live a certain way. We are called to put our trust in him.

Reflection

Take a moment to envision the nativity. Dwell on its beautiful and rich meaning. Ask yourself, "Who is Jesus to me?" Do you know him as simply a baby in a story, or is he the Savior of your soul?

Prayer

Jesus, I believe that you are the Son of God who was born, lived a holy life, died on the cross, and rose from the dead. You are the King of kings, and I am thankful that I know you as my Savior. I offer myself to you—my past, my present, and my future. I choose to live for you with all my heart, mind, and strength. Use me to bring you honor and reflect your love to others.

EXPERIENCE THE
FATHER'S TABLE

*Then he [Jesus] took the cup, and when he had given
thanks, he gave it to them, saying, "Drink from it,
all of you. This is my blood of the covenant, which is
poured out for many for the forgiveness of sins."*

—Matt. 26:27–28

*The law requires that nearly everything be cleansed
with blood, and without the shedding of blood there
is no forgiveness.*

—Heb. 9:22

When I transition a service into a time of communion, I often
liken the moment to a family reunion where people sit around
the table telling the same familiar stories and enjoying them as
if they're hearing them for the first time. In our family, one of
our favorite stories is about a time when on a walk with my girls,

our dog found a duck egg underneath a tree and brought it to me. We took it home and put it in a fish tank underneath a lamp, and in a few days, it hatched. We named the duckling Quackers and kept him until he was grown enough to live in a nearby pond with other ducks. There are many funny parts of the story that we tell over and over, each family member remembering something unique. We laugh every time we tell this family story.

Partaking in communion with other followers of Jesus is one of the most unifying acts of the church. In communion, the church family gathers around the table of grace to tell the same story about Jesus' sacrifice, and it is meaningful every time. It is more than a religious obligation. There is a sense of wonder when we remember the price paid for our salvation. When we partake as a group, we each remember the uniqueness of our experience in giving our lives to Christ, but more importantly, we remember the Christ who gave his life for us.

When I was a child, I thought the reason Jesus came was to literally save sheep from being slaughtered. When I was around nine years old, I stood up on the pew one day to give a thanksgiving testimony and said, "I thank God Jesus died on the cross so we don't have to kill animals anymore." I knew the story quite well: Jesus became the sacrificial lamb, and when Jesus died on the cross, we no longer needed to kill a lamb. It wasn't until I was older that I learned that the one Jesus came to save was me, not the sheep.

In Leviticus, when a person brought a sin sacrifice to God, they were to lay their hands on it before it was sacrificed. This act involved pressing firmly on the head of the sacrificial animal, thereby symbolically transmitting sins onto the animal (Lev. 1:4). The animal was then sacrificed and offered to God for the forgiveness of sins with the purpose of restoring a relationship with him. The sacrifice brought atonement.

The root idea of the word *atonement* is "to cover" or "to conceal," suggesting a covering that conceals a person's sins and makes it possible for him or her to approach God. The covenant relationship between God and mankind depended on the shedding of blood. The blood was not really the issue, but it represented life and death. The sin of the offender was placed on the sacrificial animal, and the animal had to die. It was the blood that sealed the transaction.

You don't have to look too hard to see the inadequacy of this system since humans are in constant need of sin offerings. Although sacrifices continued to be offered, there was no change in people's behavior. The sacrifices of the Old Testament only covered and concealed their sins, but it never took them away. They did, however, point toward a future when God would send the perfect sacrifice, a new covenant, to be offered once and for all.

Jesus ushered in a new covenant. He came to *take away sins*, not just cover them, through the sacrifice of himself. What ancient sacrifices foreshadowed, Christ accomplished. At the cross, God placed the sins of the whole world, your sins and mine, on his Son. "By one sacrifice he has made perfect forever those who are being made holy" (Heb. 10:14).

When we eat the bread during communion, we remember the body of Jesus that was broken for us so we could be made whole. When we drink the juice, we are reminded of the new covenant sealed with his blood.

Reflection

What is the story you tell of your salvation?

When did you understand the meaning of Jesus's death and resurrection?

Find a quiet space, and listen to "O the Blood" by Gateway Worship.

Prayer

Lord, remind me of my deliverance from sin. I was truly lost and
without hope, and then you rescued me. I have a new life in you.
Help me never to receive communion without reflecting on the
price you paid for my sin.

TWENTY-TWO

IIIIIIIIIIIIIIIIIIIIIIIIIIIIIIIIIIIIIIIIIIII

EXPERIENCE THE
FATHER'S SEAL

And you also were included in Christ when you heard
the message of truth, the gospel of your salvation.
When you believed, you were marked in him with a
seal, the promised Holy Spirit.

—Eph. 1:13

When Centerpointe Church entered into a contract to sell our property, we asked for a deposit that guaranteed the buyer was serious and would continue to work until the day of closure. The down payment was only a foretaste of what the future would hold. It was evidence that all the terms of the contract would be met and that the individual would follow through on their promise.

In the same way, the Holy Spirit confirms that God has begun a work in us and will continue to work in us to guarantee what is to come. When we accept Christ, God puts a deposit on us—the

Holy Spirit—in order to keep us and assure us that God will follow through on his promise and redeem his people.

I love the church too much not to include a discussion of the Holy Spirit. I believe in his person, work, and power. I have experienced his presence in my life, and it's too wonderful not to share it. As the third person of the Trinity, the Holy Spirit works with God the Father and God the Son in everything.

The Holy Spirit is the part of God that actually dwells inside us. Jesus made this deposit within us when he breathed on the disciples before his ascension. To set a seal on something is to put a mark on it that certifies authenticity or approval. When the FDA (Food and Drug Administration) puts their mark on something, it says the product, used for its intended use, is safe for consumption. God's stamp of approval is the Holy Spirit who comes to us the moment of our new birth. The *Bible Knowledge Commentary* puts it this way:

> A seal on a document in New Testament times identified it and indicated its owner, who would "protect" it. So too, in salvation, the Holy Spirit, like a seal, confirms that Christians are identified with Christ and are God's property, protected by Him. It was probably this thought that caused Paul to describe himself as a slave of Christ.[12]

What is more amazing about the Holy Spirit is that he is not just passing through. He comes to reside in us—make us his home. He is not a temporal toy but an eternal treasure. He is not

---

12. David K. Lowery, "2 Corinthians," in *The Bible Knowledge Commentary,* eds. John F. Walvoord and Roy B. Zuck, Accordance electronic edition (Wheaton: Victor Books, 1983), 2:557.

fickle and does not leave us when things get rough. Even when we choose not to listen to him, he is not going anywhere.

It is also helpful to understand that the Holy Spirit is not some external force to be called up by some emotional experience. He is a person who resides within us, confirming our relationship with Jesus and the Father. If we think of him only as a force, we will be tempted to try to use him for our purposes when the opposite should be true. He wants to use us for his purposes because we are the temple of the Holy Spirit.

R. A. Torrey wrote in his book *The Person and Work of the Holy Spirit*:

> If we think of the Holy Spirit as so many do as merely a power or influence, our constant thought will be, "How can I get more of the Holy Spirit," but if we think of him in the biblical way as a Divine Person, our thought will rather be, "How can the Holy Spirit have more of me?" The conception of the Holy Spirit as a divine influence or power that we are somehow to get a hold of and use, leads to self-exaltation and self-sufficiency. One who so thinks of the Holy Spirit and who at the same time imagines that he has received the Holy Spirit will almost inevitably be full of spiritual pride and strut about as if he belonged to some superior order of Christians.[13]

Reflection

Think about the presence of the Holy Spirit in your life. How does this presence strengthen your walk with God?

---

13. R. A. Torrey, *The Person and Work of the Holy Spirit*, Google Books.

Prayer

Holy Spirit, thank you for your presence and the security I find through you. Thank you for empowering me to live a life pleasing to the Father and the joy, hope, and strength you provide. Thank you for continually reminding me that I am a child of God.

TWENTY-THREE

EXPERIENCE THE FATHER'S COMFORT

Praise be to the God and Father of our Lord Jesus Christ, the Father of compassion and the God of all comfort, who comforts us in all our troubles, so that we can comfort those in any trouble with the comfort we ourselves receive from God. For just as we share abundantly in the sufferings of Christ, so also our comfort abounds through Christ. If we are distressed, it is for your comfort and salvation; if we are comforted, it is for your comfort, which produces in you patient endurance of the same sufferings we suffer. And our hope for you is firm, because we know that just as you share in our sufferings, so also you share in our comfort.

—2 Cor. 1:3–7

The week before Mother's Day, I called my mom to thank her for being a great mom. She was telling me how God had helped her over the years to raise my sisters and me. She asked, "Have I ever told you the story of when God put his arms around me?" When I said that she had not, she told me that as a mom with three teenage kids, she really struggled with insecurity and loneliness. She didn't know how she was going to make it. She drove us to our high school every morning and then went to work. One morning, she felt particularly overwhelmed. After dropping us off, she desperately called out to God. "God, I need your help." In that moment, she physically felt God's arms around her, giving her a warm hug. From that moment on, she knew she was not alone.

That, my friend, is the work of the Holy Spirit.

The Apostle Paul personally experienced the comfort of God in the midst of great sufferings. To express the anguish he felt, he used a number of words many of us can identify with: *tribulation, sufferings, afflicted, burdened, despaired,* and *sentence of death.* As great as he was in character and ministry, Paul was human like the rest of us, and in his greatest suffering, he experienced God's comfort.

One of the key words in 2 Corinthians is *comfort,* or *encouragement.* The Greek word means "called to one's side to help." The verb form is used 18 times in this letter, and the noun form is used 11 times. In spite of all the trials, Paul was able, by the grace of God, to write a letter saturated with encouragement.

During the 2020 COVID-19 pandemic, there were many sad stories of people, especially in elder facilities, who died without family around them. I was watching one interview with a healthcare worker who did everything she could to bring the dying comfort and communicate with family members. One of her main roles was to make sure they knew their loved ones were not alone. These care workers became the heroes of the coronavirus crisis. They put themselves in the same room as the virus in order to bring care and comfort to people in their last moments of life.

Discouragement is no respecter of persons. It comes to the successful and the struggler, and is unpredictable in how long it stays. But even in discouragement, we are not alone. The Comforter is our constant companion, drawing us into the presence of Jesus.

Reflection

When have you experienced the comforting arms of God wrapped around you?

If you are experiencing discouragement today, allow the Holy Spirit to wrap his loving arms around you.

Prayer

Holy Spirit, thank you for being with me in all things. I need your comfort today. Help me sense your loving arms around me.

TWENTY-FOUR

EXPERIENCE THE FATHER'S COUNSELOR

But the Advocate, the Holy Spirit, whom the Father will send in my name, will teach you all things and will remind you of everything I have said to you.

—John 14:26

When the Advocate comes, whom I will send to you from the Father—the Spirit of truth who goes out from the Father—he will testify about me.

—John 15:26

But very truly I tell you, it is for your good that I am going away. Unless I go away, the Advocate will not come to you; but if I go, I will send him to you.

—John 16:7

Okay, queue the lawyer joke: "What's the difference between a good lawyer and a bad lawyer? A bad lawyer might let a case drag on for several years. A good lawyer knows how to make it last even longer."[14]

We love lawyer jokes—until we need a lawyer. Then we understand their necessity. We use lawyers because they understand all the details of a matter. Recently, we were evaluating the church's bylaws and constitution. I have been through this process before and have a general idea of what I'm looking at, but I am also smart enough to ask a different set of eyes, a trained set of eyes, to review it with me. I reviewed it with our attorney, and sure enough, there were thoughts, sentences, words, and even punctuation that needed revision in order to serve the church for the future. In our relocation process, we needed lawyers to draft sales contracts, review offers, change some language, and sign contracts. It seemed endless to me. On more than one occasion, I thought the lawyers were dragging things out just to send one more invoice. But I learned some valuable lessons, primarily that words in a contract matter because once it is signed, you have to live by it. It became a guide for us and pointed out the consequences of our decisions.

In a similar way, the Holy Spirit knows all the details of our situation, and he works to guide our lives, not as a passive listener but as a proactive helper. The Holy Spirit is sometimes described in the original Greek as *parakletos* (John 14:16). This word is difficult to translate, but it is adopted from the Hebrew thought of a counselor—one who seeks God on another's behalf to bring about a resolve, or to stand with someone to lead and guide.

---

14. "20 Lawyer Jokes You Should Never Tell," *ParalegalEDU.org*, September 23, 2021, https://www.paralegaledu.org/2018/06/20-lawyer-jokes-you -should-never-tell/.

Imagine how the disciples felt when Jesus told them he was about to leave them. They must have felt like orphans. He had cared for them for three years, and now he was leaving. No more meals, no more discussions, no more free bread, no more storm calming, and no more walking on water. It must have been confusing and disillusioning. However, he promised a replacement—someone who would be in them to guide, lead, and empower them to do even greater works than they did with him.

The Holy Spirit also guides us through our own internal convictions. When I was a kid, I was told that conviction is like having a triangle inside you. When your actions are wrong, the triangle spins, and the points act as a painful signal that we should rethink what we are doing. If we ignore this signal long enough, the triangle points will wear down to a circle. When the circle spins, there is no longer any feeling of conviction. The idea here is to be sensitive to the work of the Spirit. Do not ignore his voice.

The Holy Spirit as counselor also strengthens us to make bold decisions by reminding us of God's presence. Sometimes fear of the future overcomes us. There may be no reason for it, but it is there. In that moment, we can go to the Lord and present our fear to the Holy Spirit, and he gives us the courage we need to move forward.

Reflection

Where do you need the counsel of the Holy Spirit right now? Take a minute to present your concern to him with the reminder that he is your counselor.

Prayer

Lord, thank you for being my defense. Instead of being defensive, I will lean on you to defend me. Give me guidance in this situation so that my life can bring honor to your name.

III

EXPERIENCE THE
FATHER'S HARVEST JOY

May the nations be glad and sing for joy, for you rule the peoples with equity and guide the nations of the earth. May the peoples praise you, God; may all the peoples praise you. The land yields its harvest; God, our God, blesses us. May God bless us still, so that all the ends of the earth will fear him.

—Ps. 67:4–7

Don't you have a saying, "It's still four months until harvest"? I tell you, open your eyes and look at the fields! They are ripe for harvest. Even now the one who reaps draws a wage and harvests a crop for eternal life, so that the sower and the reaper may be glad together. Thus the saying "One sows and another reaps" is true. I sent you to reap what you have not worked for. Others have done the hard work, and you have reaped the benefits of their labor.

—John 4:35–38

I tell you that in the same way there will be more rejoicing in heaven over one sinner who repents than over ninety-nine righteous persons who do not need to repent.

—Luke 15:7

When Scripture speaks of a harvest, it is referring to people giving their lives to Christ. Although I have never been a farmer, I know a little bit about harvest because my uncles were hobby farmers. They had a few acres for a few steers, and they rented a few acres to grow hay. On my grandmother's property was a little red barn, just big enough to store enough hay for the steers to last through a winter. In the spring, they planted seed; in the fall, they gathered the harvest.

I learned that first you have to prepare for the harvest by plowing the soil. Then you have to plant seeds in expectation of a harvest. Finally, you wait several months as the seeds take root and grow. During that time, you pray for rain—not so much that it floods the field and destroys the crop but enough for the plants to grow. You also get the tractor and plows ready for harvest. The worst thing that could happen is for the harvest to come and the equipment to fail.

At some point, you cut the hay. You want it to have reached its full potential but not so much that it dies. The harvest season is short. When the crop is ready, you must be ready as well. It is from farming that we get the expression "make hay while the sun shines." You can't go on vacation. You must act. If you don't, you could lose your crop. You rally help, get to work, and keep everyone involved with great intensity and urgency.

When my uncles' hay was ready, they called all my cousins to help bail. Being a hobby farmer meant that much of the work was done by hand rather than with machinery. As the tractor produced bales of hay, we walked behind, picking up the bales and loading them onto trucks. I weighed less than 100 pounds and was loading 50-pound bales of hay onto the back of a truck. Once the truck was full, we drove to the barn and stacked the hay by hand. Reaping a harvest was hard work.

Then came the best part—party time. For us, it was homemade ice cream. The uncles were proud of their harvest, and we boys felt like men—strong and powerful. We bragged about lifting the bales of hay and exaggerated their weight. A boy couldn't be happier.

It's in this same way that people come into the kingdom of God. Jesus tells us in John 4 that the fields are ripe for harvest. Harvest was the happiest time of the year in Palestine, marked by many religious festivals and feasts. Psalm 126:5–6 declares, "Those who sow in tears will reap with songs of joy. Those who go out weeping, carrying seed to sow, will return with songs of joy, carrying sheaves with them." Luke 15 tells us that there is rejoicing in heaven when a sinner repents.

Reflection

When have you had to gather something or collect something valuable to you? Can you remember the satisfaction? Imagine what it is like for God to gather what he loves the most—people. Let's celebrate together every person who comes to faith in Christ.

Prayer

Bringing in the Sheaves

Sowing in the morning, sowing seeds of kindness,
Sowing in the noontide and the dewy eve;
Waiting for the harvest, and the time of reaping,
We shall come rejoicing, bringing in the sheaves.

Refrain:

Bringing in the sheaves, bringing in the sheaves,
We shall come rejoicing, bringing in the sheaves,
Bringing in the sheaves, bringing in the sheaves,
We shall come rejoicing, bringing in the sheaves.

Sowing in the sunshine, sowing in the shadows,
Fearing neither clouds nor winter's chilling breeze;
By and by the harvest, and the labor ended,
We shall come rejoicing, bringing in the sheaves.

Going forth with weeping, sowing for the Master,
Though the loss sustained our spirit often grieves;
When our weeping's over, He will bid us welcome,
We shall come rejoicing, bringing in the sheaves.

TWENTY-SIX

||||||||||||||||||||||||||||||||||||||||||||

EXPERIENCE THE
HOLY SPIRIT'S POWER

*On one occasion, while he was eating with them, he gave
them this command: "Do not leave Jerusalem, but wait
for the gift my Father promised, which you have heard
me speak about. For John baptized with water, but in a
few days you will be baptized with the Holy Spirit."*

—Acts 1:4–5

*You will receive power when the Holy Spirit comes on
you; and you will be my witnesses in Jerusalem, and
in all Judea and Samaria, and to the ends of the earth.*

—Acts 1:8

*So the word of God spread. The number of disciples
in Jerusalem increased rapidly, and a large number of
priests became obedient to the faith.*

—Acts 6:7

I define a Pentecostal church as a Christ-centered, Bible-believing body of Christ that believes that the Holy Spirit is actively working today and that all the gifts of the Spirit listed in the New Testament are still available to us to strengthen believers and empower them to proclaim the good news to the world. Many people did not believe that the gifts of the Spirit were still in operation today, but the results are now in: millions of people around the world are coming to Christ because the power of the Holy Spirit is breaking through difficult places.

The litmus test for a Pentecostal church is not how many people speak in tongues, interpret tongues, or have extreme emotions. You may or may not have any of those things. The litmus test for a Pentecostal church is whether or not people are coming to Christ.

Before Jesus departed for heaven, he told his disciples to wait in Jerusalem until they received power from heaven. On the day of Pentecost, it happened. They received power, which resulted in a large number of people being saved. Isn't it interesting that the people closest to Jesus were not yet equipped to do the work of Jesus until they received the power of the Holy Spirit? What was true then is true today.

The word *power* in the original language is the Greek word *dunamei.* From *dunamei* we derive our words *dynamic* and *dynamite;* however, dynamite was not invented at the time of the early church. Jesus is talking about a force so powerful that it cannot be stopped. It is a divine power imparted to us through his Spirit.

The power of the Holy Spirit changed everything for the disciples. They went from deserting Jesus at the crucifixion to courageously witnessing for him, to sacrificing their own lives for him. It changed their preaching, and thousands of people converted and birthed the Christian church. Signs and wonders followed them wherever they went.

Review the last part of that purpose for the gifts of the Spirit: to strengthen believers and empower them to proclaim the good news to the world. Pentecost was and still is a feast to commemorate the grain harvest. The day of Pentecost is the day the Spirit descended upon the apostles and empowered Peter's preaching to convert thousands in Jerusalem (Acts 2).

Our inner self is the seat of influence, but it is also the seat of feebleness in our lives. We need to be strengthened with power beyond human power. We find the power and courage to face life through the Holy Spirit's working in us. When you are filled with the Holy Spirit, you will have the power to love without limits, speak without intimidation, pray without timidity, and live without fear. We don't have to wake the Holy Spirit up; rather, we need to be awakened to the work the Spirit is already doing. Our role is to partner with him and see the world through his eyes.

Pentecost today is still about the harvest—the harvest of souls.

Reflection

When have you experienced the power of the Holy Spirit working in your life?

When you think about the term *Pentecost*, what comes to mind?

Prayer

Lord, help me recognize the power of your Holy Spirit working within me. I know you are speaking and guiding, but I confess that I am not always paying attention.

TWENTY-SEVEN

IIIIIIIIIIIIIIIIIIIIIIIIIIIIIIIIIIIIIIIIIIIII

EXPERIENCE THE HOLY SPIRIT'S FRUIT

But the Holy Spirit produces this kind of fruit in our lives: love, joy, peace, patience, kindness, goodness, faithfulness, gentleness, and self-control. There is no law against these things!

—Gal. 5:22–23 NLT

On our kitchen table is a small, round, metal dish that holds a variety of fruit—bananas, oranges, tangerines, grapes, apples, peaches, grapefruit. They are snacks if you get hungry or something to grab as you go out the door. At the moment of this writing, four small oranges are in the dish and seem to have been there for a while. No doubt they will be replaced after Esther comes home from the grocery store.

Imagine for a moment that our lives are like that dish on God's table with fruit for others to enjoy as they interact with us. The fruits of the Spirit are the character traits found in our lives that reflect the nature of Christ.

Notice a key word in our passage today—*produces*. It indicates a process, not an instant reality. As we grow in our walk with Jesus, fruit naturally grows because Jesus is daily transforming our lives to be more like him. Fruit is the byproduct of Christ's control; it should naturally improve as our relationship in Christ grows.

The spiritual fruit we produce should create spiritual hunger in the hearts of unbelievers because it is from our fruit that the world gets a taste of who God is. The spiritual fruit we bear makes the unbeliever hungry for the things of God. Dr. Dell Tarr, one of my university presidents, taught that the fruit produced in our lives is for the weary travelers around us. It becomes one of the most dynamic evangelical tools God has ever created. Here's the way it works:

> When you find a weary traveler and when he says, "I am sick of the church," you say to him, "Have a grape." He takes it and tastes it. He says, "That is the sweetest thing I have ever tasted," and you invite him to take another. So when he comes struggling and limping to you and plucks a grape from your hand, he says, "Wow! That's good! You must be a real Christian."
>
> The true sweetness of service, the care, the genuine love, the giving, and sacrifice are something that blows him away because the world doesn't have it. The world is alien to this. When you are full of meekness, joy, peace, faith, and love, he will say, "Where did you get that, and where can I get some?"[15]

---

15. Personal notes from a message delivered by Dr. Dell Tarr when he was president of Assemblies of God Theological Seminary, 1992.

Although fruit is a byproduct of the work of the Holy Spirit, it does not mean we are passive. We partner with Him. Esther is from southern New Jersey where apples, melons, peaches, and tomatoes are the main produce, which makes harvest time a beautiful sight. The trees are filled with fruit, ready to be picked; however, the work of the farmer does not stop when the harvest is over. Fruit trees require constant care. Farmers are constantly monitoring the environment, the soil, the water, and the health of the tree. They are on constant watch for bugs and infectious diseases.

The farmer's job also requires the unpleasant task of pruning. Although painful to the tree and unpleasant to the eyes, farmers know that pruning the tree produces a healthier and heartier fruit. Branches that no longer bear fruit, along with weaker branches that are taking nourishment away from the rest of the tree, are cut off and disposed of.

In the same way, our Heavenly Father works in our lives in order to produce good fruit. Jesus said, "I am the true vine, and my Father is the gardener. He cuts off every branch in me that bears no fruit, while every branch that does bear fruit he prunes so that it will be even more fruitful" (John 15:1–2). Sometimes we feel as though he is taking things away from us, but in reality, he is working in us a more abundant life.

Reflection

How is the fruit of the Spirit in your life attracting others to Jesus?

In what ways has the Lord worked in your past to produce healthy fruit?

What is the Lord asking you to adjust in order to produce more healthy fruit?

Prayer

Lord, may my life bear fruit that attracts people to the abundant life you have for all of us. I am open to your Holy Spirit's inspection of my life. Help me recognize the areas you want to prune so I can be more effective in your kingdom. Although the process might be painful, the joy of the finished product outweighs the discomfort I presently feel.

TWENTY-EIGHT

EXPERIENCE THE HOLY SPIRIT'S GIFTS

We have different gifts, according to the grace given to each of us. If your gift is prophesying, then prophesy in accordance with your faith; if it is serving, then serve; if it is teaching, then teach; if it is to encourage, then give encouragement; if it is giving, then give generously; if it is to lead, do it diligently; if it is to show mercy, do it cheerfully.

—Rom. 12:6–8

It takes all the people of God, experiencing all the gifts of God, to do all the work of God.

I was awake at 3:00 a.m., sitting in my recliner complaining to God, and struggling with disappointment. It was immature for sure, but it bothered me enough that I could no longer sleep. As I sat in my pity party, God was not pleased, and he let me know it. Like a father disciplines his son, he clearly said to me, "You can

continue to sit there and sulk, but you are cursing and not blessing. I have given you gifts that can bless the situation, but you are
choosing to curse." It broke my heart to think about how childish
I had become. I had a decision to make: I could use my gifts, or
I could withhold them. That morning I drafted a letter and sent
it, offering support and whatever gifts I had, and was wonder-
fully surprised that the person took me up on my offer. Just a few
months later, I was asked to serve on the same board I had com-
plained about. The Lord had prepared me over the years for this
moment and then prepared my heart in a moment of repentance.

God has uniquely gifted each of us by the Holy Spirit to be
a blessing to the body of Christ, our community, and the world.
Instead of withholding our gifts, we must steward and use them
for the kingdom. We all have a choice to make. We can use our
gifts only by offering them to God and others. All gifts must bring
glory to Jesus, build up the body of Christ, and empower us to
reach the world for Christ.

Romans 12:6–8, Ephesians 4:11–13, and 1 Corinthians 12:7–
11 list the spiritual gifts, which are categorized as follows:

Leadership gifts: apostles, prophets, evangelists,
pastors, teachers (also called the five-fold ministry
gifts)

Verbal gifts: preaching, teaching, prophesying,
evangelizing, speaking in tongues, interpreting
tongues

Manifestation gifts: prophecy, faith, miracles, healing

Serving gifts: generosity, hospitality, encouragement

Some gifts are definitely more expressive and prominent, but none are more significant than others. Whatever gifts we have, we must steward and strengthen within the context of a community of love.

The Corinthian church was obsessed with the value of spiritual gifts, equating the social status of a gift with the significance of the one who possessed it. That was Paul's concern. First Corinthians 13 gives specific treatment to three gifts: tongues, prophecy, and knowledge. These religious activities, many of them from the list in 1 Corinthians 12:8–10, do not benefit the person doing them if that person's life is not characterized by love or if they are so caught up in certain spiritual gifts that they have unconsciously abandoned true love.

Paul tells us that any gift, even exercised to its highest level of performance, has diminished value if it is exercised without love. Spiritual gifts, as wonderful as they are, can never be a substitute for love; instead, they empower you to serve others.

Reflection

What are your spiritual gifts, and how did you discover them? For a list of spiritual gifts, read Ephesians 4:11–13 and 1 Corinthians 12:7–11.

How are your spiritual gifts helpful in your life?

How are you using your spiritual gifts to serve others?

What are ways you can nurture the gifts God has given you?

Prayer

Lord, I am grateful for the gifts you have given me. Today, I will honor you by using my gifts to serve others.

Through is a helping word, a preposition that expresses a relationship to something else. We go through a door that connects us to another room. We pass through a toll booth that takes us from one state to another. In this section, we will experience God through some spiritual disciplines. They are gateways that help us in our spiritual formation.

We know that there is nothing we can do to make God love us more. He offers his love and grace to us unconditionally. We do not get to heaven by works, acts of compassion, generosity, Bible memorization, church attendance, mission trips, or according to how many people we witnessed to last week. We get to heaven simply by confessing with our mouths and believing in our hearts that God raised Jesus from the dead (Rom. 10:9). However, we are still left with this question: How do we actually live out our faith in practical ways?

Through reading and meditating on his Word, worshiping, praying, and giving, we grow in the grace and knowledge of the one we love. Our hearts are strengthened, and our understanding of him deepens. None of these make God love us more. We practice them out of our desire to know God's amazing grace in a more profound way.

SECTION TWO

THE COMMUNITY OF A
JESUS-FOLLOWER

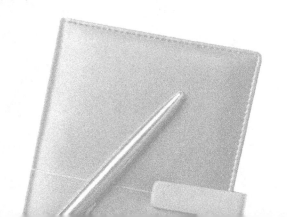

TWENTY-NINE

||||||||||||||||||||||||||||||||||||||||||||||

EXPERIENCE GOD
THROUGH HIS CHURCH

Let us hold unswervingly to the hope we profess, for he who promised is faithful. And let us consider how we may spur one another on toward love and good deeds, not giving up meeting together, as some are in the habit of doing, but encouraging one another—and all the more as you see the Day approaching.

—Heb. 10:23–25

Saying you don't need to be part of a church is like saying you don't need to be on a team in order to play baseball. You technically can. I did all the time as a kid. The church next to my house provided a wonderful wall where I practiced throwing. I also went in my backyard and threw the ball as far I as I could and then ran after it to practice catching. Even so, I still was not playing baseball until I was playing the game with eight other teammates.

When I hear people say, "I don't need the church to be a Christian," "I don't need the church to be saved," "I don't believe in organized religion," "We don't need to come to a building to have church," or "I can experience church at home," I am deeply saddened—but not because of the technical accuracy. It is true; you don't *need* to go to a building to be in church. I am saddened because, in my experience, these statements usually come from a place of pain, discomfort, or disappointment.

The biggest misconception among believers about the church is the thought, "I am the church." This is a popular thought, and it sounds so spiritual, but it is simply not true. You (singular) are not the church. I am not the church. *We* are the church. I can pray alone. I can read alone. I can study alone. But none of those things make me the body of Christ.

We need a higher view of the church, one that is biblical and hopeful. The church is set in the context of a broken and needy world in order to show a better way. The church is a family on a mission to invite people to meet Jesus, help them grow in their faith, develop them for service, and send them out to transform the community. In *A Radical Idea: Unleashing the People of God for the Purpose of God*, David Platt wrote:

> If you and I want our lives to count for God's purpose in the world, we need to begin with a commitment to God's people in the church. God has called us to lock arms with one another in single-minded, death-defying obedience to one objective: the declaration of his gospel for the demonstration of his glory to all nations. This is God's design for his people, and it is worth giving our lives to see it accomplished. It is worth it for billions of people who do not yet know that Jesus is the grave-

conquering, life-giving, all-satisfying King. And it is worth it for you and me, because we were made to enjoy the great pleasures of God in the context of total abandonment to his global purpose.[16]

Read the admonition of the writer of Hebrews. First, we must tenaciously hold to the hope we profess so there is no doubt in God's faithfulness. Second, we must intentionally spur one another to love and good works. Third, the writer offers a slight rebuke: "not giving up meeting together, as some are in the habit of doing." This rebuke could certainly be written today. Keeping oneself from the church is a habit with lasting consequences for the whole family. Finally, encourage each other. One way to encourage each other is to simply show up. Be present. The body of Christ needs you, especially today when others are lessening their commitment.

If you are not being spiritually fed at church, as people often say, bring some food with you, and share it with others. In other words, listen to the writer of Hebrews, and bring value and encouragement with you. Be part of the solution; don't create a relational vacuum.

Reflection

What is your relationship in the body of Christ? Are you active, or have you gone missing in action?

What are ways you can encourage someone in the context of community?

---

16. David Platt, *A Radical Idea: Unleashing the People of God for the Purpose of God* (Colorado Springs: Multnomah Books, 2011), 6–7.

Prayer

Lord, help me see the body of Christ the way you do. Speak to me about my attitude, my role, my relationships, and my participation. I do not want to withhold anything from you or my fellow believers.

THIRTY

EXPERIENCE GOD THROUGH COMMUNITY

All the believers were one in heart and mind. No one claimed that any of their possessions was his own, but they shared everything they had. With great power the apostles continued to testify to the resurrection of the Lord Jesus. And God's grace was so powerfully at work in them all.

—Acts 4:32–33

We cannot fulfill God's purposes for our lives by ourselves. There's no way we can be all God wants us to be, do all God wants us to do, or fulfill our God-given purposes by ourselves. We need relationships with other people. We need each other, and we belong to each other in the body of Christ.

The church is intensely relational. Look at the metaphors Scripture uses concerning the church. The church is called the body of Christ (Rom. 12:5; 1 Cor. 12:27; Eph. 1:23). It is also called the bride of Christ (Rev. 19:7; 21:2, 9, 22:17). Both images describe an intimate connection between one thing and another.

Today, church has become an option in people's mind, and they show up only when it is convenient. They get their messages from online media resources and call them "church." The church has responded, and I don't blame them, by putting their services online. The problem is that there are some things you can't download—encouragement is one of them. We may be able to post a sad emoji next to a discouraging comment or a happy one next to someone's vacation, but we can't replace someone looking us in the eyes and speaking words of hope.

Communities offer safety. Have you ever taken a walk in an unfamiliar place, a dark alley at night, or a path in the woods? Walking alone can be a little disconcerting. In the Psalms, there is a section called the Psalms of Ascent. As the Israelites traveled to Jerusalem for worship, they traveled together, in community, because the trip was dangerous. They talked and sang songs together to give encouragement and security. There was safety in numbers.

Have you ever watched a lion stalk a herd of zebras or impalas? One way to catch prey is to separate an animal from its herd. They can even kill one of the larger animals if they get it alone. Such is the best way Satan can pick us off—when we are alone.

Being in community also keeps us from giving up because community is supportive. When you're walking with other people, you gain the energy and motivation to keep on going. There's an old Zambian proverb that says, "When you run alone, you run fast. But when you run together, you run far." Those are good words. Life is not a 50-yard dash; it is a marathon. You want to make it to the end of life, and the only way to make it there the way God wants you to is by involving others in your life.

It is also smarter to stay in community. You learn more by walking with others than by walking alone. Proverbs 28:26 (CEV) says, "Only fools would trust what they alone think." In other words, if I'm the only one who thinks this, and nobody else agrees with me, guess what? I'm wrong. You may be walking in the wrong direction. But if you're walking by yourself through life, you have no one to say, "We're off the path. We missed it. We've got to get back on the path." Isolation leads us to many false and troublesome places. The Bible tells us, "In an abundance of counselors there is safety" (Prov. 11:14 ESV). We need others to watch out for our lives—people who will defend, stand up for, protect, and feed us. We all have blind spots, but if we are looking out for the interest of others, we are protected.

Deep in the human spirit is a longing for belonging. This longing is the reason solitary confinement is the worst kind of punishment. We were made for relationships. God wired us that way. People will join all kinds of causes just because they want to belong. The people in your neighborhood would love to come to your house.

Reflection

What does your community look like? If you are having difficulty connecting with your community, find an area to serve. Be the community you want to be part of.

Prayer

Lord, help me love my community more than ever. Open my eyes to see how I can come alongside others with support and love.

THIRTY-ONE

IIIIIIIIIIIIIIIIIIIIIIIIIIIIIIIIIIIIIIIIIIIII

EXPERIENCE GOD THROUGH CONFESSION

If you enter your place of worship and, about to make an offering, you suddenly remember a grudge a friend has against you, abandon your offering, leave immediately, go to this friend and make things right. Then and only then, come back and work things out with God.

—Matt. 5:24 MSG

I'm sorry are some of the most important words in the human language, but they are also some of the most difficult words to utter. They do not roll off the tongue easily, and they are bitter to the taste, but in them contain freedom and healing. Asking for forgiveness is like eating humble pie, and the taste of humble pie is sickening to your stomach.

I have had to confess my offenses to others many times, and each time was an unpleasant but completely necessary experience for my spiritual and emotional wholeness. In some cases, I carried deep-seated regrets for a while, and being reminded of the confession moment was a reminder of God's grace and restoration. The words *I'm sorry* begin the process. If we want relationships to honor God, someone has to take the first step.

Confessions are especially relevant in family relationships because we generally hurt deepest the people who are closest to us. Movies may succeed with the idea that love is "never having to say you're sorry," but I've never known a family to succeed on that premise. Most family members have to say "I'm sorry" a great deal.

Sitting in my office on a Friday afternoon, I bowed my head in prayer and asked, "Is there anything you want to talk to me about?" I had just completed a sermon on forgiveness. God's voice was not audible, but it was powerful. He said, "Since you asked, you need to call someone and ask forgiveness." I knew who he was talking about and finally surrendered. I picked up the phone and made the call, hoping no one would answer so I could simply leave a message. To my surprise, the person answered the phone. We talked for a few minutes, and then I shared that I had been convicted by God to call and simply say, "I'm sorry." I had put off making the call for a long time because, in comparison, I felt the issue was more the other person's than mine, but that didn't matter. I had the responsibility to confess.

As we continued to talk, the person extended grace, and I felt it immediately. Months later, I ran into that person and could confidently chat without reservation. If it weren't for that phone call, I'd have wanted to hide under a chair when the person walked in the room.

To seek forgiveness means to humbly acknowledge what you did wrong and take complete responsibility for your actions and words. Pride and confession can't coexist.

In Matthew 5, Jesus said we are to immediately set aside our offering, an act of worship, to make things right. I love this story about Winston Churchill and his wife:

At a dinner party one night Lady Churchill was seated across the table from Sir Winston, who kept making his hand walk up and down—two fingers bent at the knuckles. The fingers appeared to be walking toward Lady Churchill. Finally, her dinner partner asked, "Why is Sir Winston looking at you so wistfully, and whatever is he doing with those knuckles on the table?" "That's simple," she replied. "We had a mild quarrel before we left home, and he is indicating it's his fault and he's on his knees to me in abject apology."[17]

Reflection

Do you have any relationships that are fractured because of something you said or did? What prevents you from asking for forgiveness?

Prayer

Lord, as much as it hurts, I need to ask forgiveness of someone I have wounded. Please go before me, and prepare the way. Give me wisdom and courage to face my responsibility.

---

17. Linda Dillow, *What's It Like to Be Married to Me? And Other Dangerous Questions* (Colorado Springs: David C. Cook, 2011), 163.

THIRTY-TWO

EXPERIENCE GOD THROUGH FORGIVENESS

Forgive us our sins, for we also forgive everyone who sins against us.

—Luke 11:4

If your brother or sister sins against you, rebuke them; and if they repent, forgive them. Even if they sin against you seven times in a day and seven times come back to you saying "I repent," you must forgive them.

—Luke 17:3–4

Jesus said, "Father, forgive them, for they do not know what they are doing." And they divided up his clothes by casting lots.

—Luke 23:34

The other side of repentance is the ability to extend forgiveness. Yes, it happened. Certainly it hurt, and it may still hurt, but at some point, we must forgive. Some wounds are deep. They hurt more than we realize and stir up intense anger and lasting bitterness. We blame not only the offender but also anyone who remotely resembles them. Only God can give us the grace to forgive and move past the offenses.

Forgiveness is an expression of love, and it looks like Jesus. It is the most Christlike action we are asked to do. Jesus looked down on the ones who crucified him and said, "Forgive them, for they do not know what they are doing." When people forgive, they are a true light to a sinful world.

Forgiveness is a sacrifice. It is likely that old wounds will resurface, even things you thought you'd let go of years ago, because forgiveness draws out deep memories. These memories can actually be a gift from God since they remind us of moments when God helped us and assured us that he will be with us again.

Forgiveness is a gift. It is a gift from God and will be a gift from us as we extend it to others.

I have a pastor friend who experienced major offenses from his father. He could have easily taken his bitterness and hatred to his grave and let his dad experience his anger in his last days, but by God's grace, he was able to forgive. In a Facebook post, he reflected on his experience, and he agreed to let me share it. Here's what he wrote:

Reflections, for whatever it's worth . . .

In his last days, my father called my name as I was walking out of his hospital room ready to leave. I turned around and he looked at me as best as his 10%

vision could see me and said, "I'm sorry I wasn't the best father I could be for you. I know I could've done better." This man who had beat my mother regularly, stolen money from me, even the inheritance that my grandmother left for me, and walked out on our family while I was a junior in college, leaving my mom and sisters to be evicted and fend on their own, had been filled with regret as he surveyed his life and knew his days were numbered. My response: I walked over to him with tear filled eyes, kissed his forehead and said "Daddy, I love you, you are forgiven, be at peace." Subsequently, a few months later, I would cry, hug and kiss his forehead repeatedly as I was led back to the room where his dead body lay at Good Samaritan hospital. My only prayer and wish to God was that he wouldn't have to be alone in his death. God granted me the gift of being with him on his last day before he left this earth. Our last act together was eating a crab cake and praying together.[18]

Lest you think I am making forgiveness seem too simple, I can assure you I am not. When we are hurt by people close to us, the wounds go deep, and the process of forgiveness is painful and long. Forgiveness takes time and tremendous courage, and sometimes it isn't reciprocated, making the process even more painful. Forgiveness doesn't guarantee restoration of the relationship. When someone slams your hand in the door, you're required to forgive, but you don't have to put your hand back in

18. Rev. Gavin Brown, "Reflections, for whatever it's worth . . . ," Facebook, October 5, 2019.

the door. In Genesis, Esau forgave Jacob for deceiving him and taking his birthright and blessing, but the brothers never lived in the same territory again. That can be very freeing for many people.

The choice is ours. We can choose to remain bitter, or we can choose to forgive.

Reflection

What deep wound do you need God's grace to forgive?

Prayer

Dear Lord, on my own there is no way for me to forgive this offense, so I really need your help. Even praying about it hurts. I want to forgive, but it is difficult. To forgive, I feel exposed, but I need to be set free from this fear. Today, I choose to walk in forgiveness, and with your help, I will choose it again tomorrow and the next day and the next day. . . .

SECTION THREE

THE DISCIPLINES OF A
JESUS-FOLLOWER

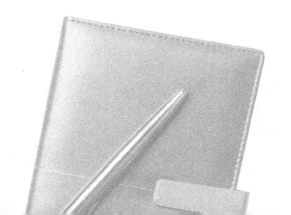

THIRTY-THREE

EXPERIENCE GOD THROUGH HIS WORD

For the word of God is living and active. Sharper than any double-edged sword, it penetrates even to dividing soul and spirit, joints and marrow; it judges the thoughts and attitudes of the heart.

—Heb. 4:12

How can a young person stay on the path of purity? By living according to your word.

—Ps. 119:9

I have hidden your word in my heart that I might not sin against you.

—Ps. 119:11

I delight in your decrees; I will not neglect your word.

—Ps. 119:16

On October 17, 2019, I had the special honor of preaching at the funeral of Lu Washington. A week before the funeral, in preparation for the service, I met with her three daughters and talked about her life. They happened to bring her Bible with them. It was a hardcover Good News Bible. From what I could tell, she received it around 1985. She must have always kept it with her because the pages were mostly detached from the binder. Her Bible tells her story of her faith. It is highlighted, underlined, and annotated with her personal notes. There was no doubt that she not only read it but also devoured it. I could almost sense her painful times from the highlighted passages that spoke of God's comfort. I could also feel the times when God spoke directly to her about a situation. At the top of the first blank page she wrote, "Help in Time of Need, Guide on Bible Passage, 1986." Here is what followed:

The Way of Salvation: John 14:16; Acts 16:31; Romans 10:9

Comfort in Loneliness: Psa. 23; Is. 41:10; Heb. 13:5, 6

Comfort in Sorrow: 2 Cor. 1:3–5; Rom. 8:26–28

Relief in Suffering: 2 Cor. 12:8–10; Heb. 12:3–13

Guidance in decision: James 1:5, 6; Pro. 3:5, 6

Help in Danger: Ps. 91, Ps. 121

Courage in fear: Heb. 13:5, 6; Eph. 6:10–18

Peace in Turmoil: Is. 26:3, 4; Phil. 4:6, 7

Rest in Weariness: Matt. 11:28, 29; Ps. 23

Strength in Temptation: James 1:12–16; 1 Cor. 10:6–13

Warning in Indifference: Gal. 5:19–21; Heb. 10:26–31

Forgiveness in Time of Correction: Is. 1:8; 1 John 1:7–9

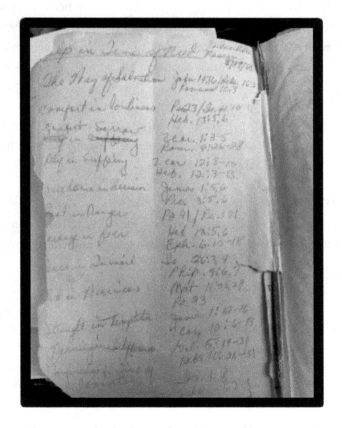

On the cover, she had taped a picture of legacy missionaries

Mike and Kay Zello, a picture that speaks to her love for missions.

She obviously loved the Psalms, Proverbs, and the book of Hebrews, but she had highlighted something in almost every book of the Bible. She had worn this Bible out. I was reminded that a Bible that is worn out is usually owned by someone who isn't.

The Bible was not just a book to Miss Lu; it was her guide and source of inner strength. The psalmist put it this way: "Your word is a lamp for my feet, a light on my path" (Ps. 119:105). I think Miss Lu was onto something. A few days before her homegoing, we prayed together, sang together, read Scripture together, and wept with the family. Then she went to meet the one she loved so much and had read so much about.

Reflection

How is your Scripture reading going? Are you as in love with God's Word as Miss Lu was? What needs to change in your life so you will prioritize the reading of God's Word?

Prayer

Dear Lord, I pray that your Word becomes alive in me. I don't just want to read it; I want it to penetrate my heart and change my life.

‖‖‖‖‖‖‖‖‖‖‖‖‖‖‖‖‖‖‖‖‖‖‖‖‖‖‖‖‖‖‖

THIRTY-FOUR

EXPERIENCE GOD THROUGH MEDITATION

Abide in me, and I in you. As the branch cannot bear fruit by itself, unless it abides in the vine, neither can you, unless you abide in me. I am the vine; you are the branches. Whoever abides in me and I in him, he it is that bears much fruit, for apart from me you can do nothing. If anyone does not abide in me he is thrown away like a branch and withers; and the branches are gathered, thrown into the fire, and burned. If you abide in me, and my words abide in you, ask whatever you wish, and it will be done for you. By this my Father is glorified, that you bear much fruit and so prove to be my disciples. As the Father has loved me, so have I loved you. Abide in my love. If you keep my commandments, you will abide in my love, just as I have kept my Father's commandments and abide in his love. These things I have spoken to you, that my joy may be in you, and that your joy may be full.

—John 15:4–11 ESV

Jesus was extremely busy, always sought after for one reason or another. He ministered to thousands. He had feeding programs, personal evangelism seminars, a much-demanded teaching ministry, a healing ministry, and a prophetic ministry. People followed him everywhere and even forced themselves on him. They would do anything to get a piece of him.

Luke 5:15–16 tells us, "Yet the news about him spread all the more, so that crowds of people came to hear him and to be healed of their sicknesses. But Jesus often withdrew to lonely places and prayed."

Sometimes Jesus withdrew on a boat or in a garden to pray. He did not withdraw because his love for people had diminished but rather to refresh his soul. He needed a break. He needed to hear the voice of his Father again. Only by a consistent pattern of quiet could he maintain balance in his life and accomplish his life's mission.

Jesus was intentional about carving out time to pray. It seems in Scripture that the more hectic his schedule, the more time he deliberately and intentionally set aside to pray.

We, on the other hand, feel as though we don't have any time for God because life is too busy. A life without prayer guarantees a powerless living. If we are going to successfully navigate through this rat race, we must spend time with our Heavenly Father.

The imperative of today's passage is *abide*, the secret to a successful Christian life. In other words, abiding is not a suggestion or just another good idea. In order to bear fruit, we must stay attached to Jesus. We need to create space for him that leads to purification, direction, wisdom, discernment, and a heart for the lost.

When I talk about getting alone with God, I am not suggesting that we reduce devotions to a ritual without substance. Contrary to popular belief, a chapter a day does not keep the devil away. We tend to think that we must spend an hour with God a day in order to make it through the day. That may be wonderful, but it also may be a clock-watching time rather than a truly relational time with God.

We tend to quantify everything, including our relationship with God. If we believe that spending 15 minutes in devotions is good, then surely 30 minutes is "gooder," and 60 minutes is "goodest" (pardon my grammar). It then becomes the time itself that makes us closer to God and not the conversation. Granted, you cannot have quality without some sort of quantity, but quantity is not the ultimate goal.

I first learned to have devotions early in the morning while I was in Bible college, and it was not for spiritual reasons. I went to a school where one water boiler served the whole school, so the hot water ran out within the first two hours of showers, and the guys had one open shower for each floor. I didn't enjoy group showers in high school, and I certainly didn't want them in college. Besides that, I just don't interact with people well before I have my coffee, and I had no access to some until breakfast was served. My only option was to get up first, so I did. After my shower, I read Scripture and prayed, which became a pattern for the rest of my life. Those moments with God are now precious to me. Sometimes I don't feel particularly inspired, but other times I have a deep sense of God's speaking to me.

Don't fall into a ritual devotional life based on works. Consider it like getting together with a close friend. Sometimes you say, "I just need to check in with you today. I need your help in this. What does your letter have to say to me, and what does your Spirit have to teach me? Here is what's happening in my life, and I wonder if you have any input you would like to share with me. If I don't get a handle on the whole thing, at least I'll know if you are with me."

Other times you meet with that friend, and the conversation is so wonderful that you can't get away. You even find yourself saying, "Oh my, look at the time. I've got to run, but let's continue this conversation later."

You see, it's not about minutes; it's about a person.

Reflection

What does your devotional life look like? Are you creating space in your life for God to change you? If you sense you need to create more space for God, what steps can you take to do that?

Prayer

Lord, today I am creating space for you to speak to me. Please help me prioritize your presence so it becomes something I cannot miss.

THIRTY-FIVE

EXPERIENCE GOD THROUGH REST

*Come to me, all you who are weary and burdened,
and I will give you rest.*

—Matt. 11:28

Be still, and know that I am God.

—Ps. 46:10

I will refresh the weary and satisfy the faint.

—Jer. 31:25

We were tired and needed a break. We needed to be together and unwind, so seven of us—all pastors—rented a house in Florida for a week. As best we can remember, we have been meeting every year for the last 18 years to talk about ministry and life. We usually had somewhat of an agenda, ate a few meals, and rented a room to talk. This year was different because no one wanted to make a decision. The COVID-19 crisis, along with the racial and political divide, drove each of us into a nonstop, decision-making mode with the potential for someone questioning the decisions we made. It was exhausting. All any of us wanted to do was rest, laugh, tell stories, and eat; so that's just what we did. It must have been said a dozen times, "I just wanted to come and not make any decisions."

I am well aware that pastors are not the only ones who have the potential to live life exhausted. Our healthcare workers are just one of a host of other professionals who are stretched to their limits. If we are not careful, the pace of and lack of space in life can dry up our emotional, physical, and spiritual lives. That can cause us to miss precious moments of God's presence and his call to come to him and find rest.

When Jesus said, "Come to me, all you who are weary and burdened, and I will give you rest," he was talking to people who had grown weary from working for the Roman government and were burdened by their own religious leaders to follow rules that led to a false sense of righteousness and led to more guilt than fulfillment.

The New Testament word *rest* comes from the Old Testament word *Sabbath*, which is an intentional time set aside to celebrate God, to experience his peace, and to remember that he is in control. Many people neglect this sacred area of life because it seems counterproductive, but those who take time for spiritual renewal on a regular basis have more energy and durability than those who do not.

Dr. Caroline Leaf, a communication pathologist and audiologist who has worked in cognitive neuroscience and pioneered work on neuroplasticity (changing our thinking actually changes the brain), wrote the fascinating and insightful book

Switch On Your Brain. In it she describes the activity of the brain during intentional times of rest. When we rest, we are actually switching on a mode of thinking that gives perspective and wisdom and the opportunity to connect with God. She wrote this in her book:

> So when our brain enters the rest circuit, we don't actually rest; we move into a highly intelligent, self-reflective, directed state. And the more often we go there, the more we get in touch with the deep, spiritual part of who we are. I believe God has created this state to directly connect us to him and to develop and practice an awareness of his presence. . . .
>
> It's a directed, deeply intellectual focusing inward and tuning out the outside world. It is a cessation from active external, which is like the Sabbath when we switch off from the world and focus on God. . . .
>
> In the busyness of life and the flurry of everyday activity, we expose ourselves to the possibility of developing a chaotic mindset with the net result of neurochemical and electromagnetic chaos in the brain. This feels like endless loops and spirals of thinking that can easily get out of control.[19]

When we rest in God, we invite the Holy Spirit to bring perspective to the issues in our life. Times of rest must be intentionally created through daily and weekly routines. Set aside

---

19. Caroline Leaf, *Switch On Your Brain* (Grand Rapids, MI: Baker Books, 2013), 82, 83, 85.

time daily to be alone with God and his Word and weekly to be in a community of worship and growth. Creating this space allows God to refresh us and speak to us.

Reflection

Tired? This may be a good day to take a nap.

Prayer

God, today I choose to rest in you. I release all my cares on you, knowing that you care for me. I choose to dwell on your goodness, your provision, your love, and your grace. As I stay in your presence, help me gain your perspective on my life and current situation.

THIRTY-SIX

EXPERIENCE GOD THROUGH PRAYER

When he had finished praying, Jesus left with his disciples and crossed the Kidron Valley. On the other side there was a garden, and he and his disciples went into it. Now Judas, who betrayed him, knew the place, because Jesus had often met there with his disciples (emphasis added).

—John 18:1–2

Scripture repeatedly reminds us of the need for prayer. We are to pray and not give up. We are to approach God with confidence (1 John 5:14–15). We are to ask, seek, and knock. If anyone is sick, they should pray. Jesus taught his disciples to pray. With thanksgiving, we are to present our requests to God (Phil. 4). Even more than the commands to pray, Scripture gives examples of all the major characters and their prayer lives.

Not many would argue against prayer. More often we face argument against committing to the discipline of prayer. We can't seem to fit it into our busy schedules. My biggest challenges regarding prayer are distractions and my pressing need to get things done. I almost feel guilty for praying because I am not accomplishing something—a faulty thinking for sure.

On the night Jesus was betrayed, Judas knew exactly where to find him because Jesus had often met there with the disciples for prayer. If you think Jesus did not have pressure, think again. He did not sit on the seashore telling parables all day long. He preached, healed, fed, ministered, got tired, and traveled with some pretty unpolished disciples. Still, he made time to pray. If Jesus, the Son of God, created time to pray, we would be wise to follow his example.

Another challenge for many is that they do not have a structure for prayer. There are many prayer models available today. Jesus presented a model for prayer in Matthew 6. I find that most prayer models have the same goal in mind, to spend time communicating with the God of the universe concerning specific matters. Let me offer to you my pattern for prayer, not as a prescription but as a description that will inform your own. We are all wired differently and must find what fits us, but it's important to start somewhere and continually develop this essential area.

My typical prayer time starts with thanksgiving and a recognition of who God is, much like the Lord's prayer. "Our Father which art in heaven, Hallowed be thy name" (Matt. 6:9 KJV). I then pray through the Scripture I am studying and ask God to work in me and speak to me according to his Word. This practice generally leads me to a prayer of confession where I ask God if there are any sin issues, offenses, unforgiveness, or places of bitterness he needs to expose. In Psalm 139:23–24, David says, "Search me, God, and know my heart; test me and know my anxious thoughts. See if there is any offensive way in me, and lead me in the way everlasting."

I then place my personal concerns before him and follow Peter's words to cast all my cares or anxieties on him (1 Pet. 5:7).

Finally, I present my requests. I like to pray in categories that are listed as cards in my Logos Bible software and in my journal. They include family, missionaries, Centerpointe Church, Potomac Ministry Network, leadership, the lost. These cards have subcategories that include people and subjects. Sometimes I pray systematically through the cards, and other times I stay on one card. My prayer is simple: "Lord, I place each area of concern before you today."

Often the Holy Spirit guides me to spend more time praying for a specific issue or person. I want to hear from God as much as I want to tell him what I want, so I need to be still and listen. Many times, God gives a Scripture, a song, a word of wisdom, or a simple thought for me to meditate on. What I do with that varies. I may simply need to trust him more. Sometimes God calls me to participate in the answer. There have been times when God has asked me to call someone or send an email or a note of encouragement. Other times he has asked me to do something more extreme. When that happens, the Holy Spirit is going before me and preparing the way as I simply partner with him in his work. Finally, I pray about my day, the people I will meet, and the tasks I will perform. When I am finished, I place my trust in God.

The rewards of creating space is not checking off your spiritual box for the day; it is spending time with your Savior and fixing your eyes on him, the author and perfecter of your faith.

Reflection

Do you have a pattern of prayer? What does it look like? Is there anything you need to change to enhance your prayer life?

Prayer

God, I desire to know you, and I realize I need to create space in my life for prayer and for listening to your voice. As I place before you the needs on my prayer list, I do so with boldness and confidence that you will hear and respond. No need is too great or too insignificant for you.

THIRTY-SEVEN

EXPERIENCE GOD
THROUGH WORSHIP

*Come, let us sing for joy to the Lord; let us shout
aloud to the Rock of our salvation. Let us come before
him with thanksgiving and extol him with music and
song. For the Lord is the great God, the great King
above all gods. In his hand are the depths of the earth,
and the mountain peaks belong to him. The sea is his,
for he made it, and his hands formed the dry land.
Come, let us bow down in worship, let us kneel before
the Lord our Maker; for he is our God and we are the
people of his pasture, the flock under his care.*

—Ps. 95:1–7

As a youth and music major in college, I was asked to lead many
worship services for chapel. In my senior year, my first official
ministry position came when I accepted an offer to lead a choir
and Sunday morning worship for a church in Pennsylvania.
When Esther and I married, we served in two churches as youth

and music pastors. Esther played the piano and led the choirs, and I led the youth and worship services. Those were great seasons for us, and we were able to encourage people to come into God's presence and worship him. Those were formative years that shaped our thoughts on worship.

It's important to understand that worship is so much more than music and singing. The church is full of consumers, and one of the biggest commodities is worship. It has become one of the biggest entertainment businesses in church life. The problem is that the church is not in the entertainment business, nor should it be. It is in the transformation business. True worship is not about the style of music we sing but the style of life we live.

Archbishop and theologian William Temple wrote, "To worship is to quicken the conscience by the holiness of God, to feed the mind with the truth of God, to purge the imagination by the beauty of God, to open the heart to the love of God, to devote the will to the purpose of God."[20]

That said, worship through music is powerful and inspiring. When I pastored a church in West Virginia, I wondered if anything would ever change and if we would ever see people come to Christ. I didn't want to pastor a church that didn't see people transformed by God. One day, I discovered the Brooklyn Tabernacle Choir. Somehow, I received a VHS copy of one of their first recorded choir productions. The first time I watched it, I wept. It showed testimonies of people who had suffered addiction and pain, had come to the church, and had been radically saved. I wanted the same experience for our church. For almost two years,

---

20. "Archbishop, Theologian, Reformer: 9 Quotes from William Temple," *Christianity Today*, November 6, 2018, https://www.christiantoday.com/article/archbishop-theologian-reformer-9-quotes-from-william-temple/130871.htm.

I woke up on Sunday mornings and watched that video recording. I knew every word and testimony, and I worshiped, believing God that one day I would see it happen.

Scripture is filled with exhortations to worship the Lord with singing, clapping, dancing, shouting, praising, and praying. The act of singing in worship is profound in our lives. The music remains in our hearts and minds long after the service is over. When we are worshiping the Lord, we turn our eyes upon him and find that the concerns of our hearts are strangely dimmed.

In my late teens and early 20s, I had a few relationship breakups. Some I had initiated, and some were initiated for me. Both ways were painful. I often got in my car, went for a ride, and listened to old love songs. My guess is that right now you are thinking of one. It takes you back to sad times. Music is powerful that way. As I look back on those depressing moments, I realize I was simply emotionally medicating myself, and it was not good. I wish I'd known then that if I had simply changed the playlist on my music, I would have been far better off, and the pain would not have lasted as long.

Most of us have a playlist, whether literally or figuratively. Perhaps we have specific stations on Pandora or Spotify that are tied to a specific artist or genre that stirs up certain emotions. When I run, I have a playlist that gets me started and keeps me going. I have a playlist for travel and a playlist for prayer.

Reflection

What is on your playlist? How much of it is uplifting, God-focused, joy-giving, and inspirational? Maybe it's time to change.

Prayer

Lord, I choose this day to worship you. May my life be an act of worship, and may my song be an act of praise.

THIRTY-EIGHT
||||||||||||||||||||||||||||||||||||||||||

EXPERIENCE GOD THROUGH GENEROSITY, PART 1

Remember this: Whoever sows sparingly will also reap sparingly, and whoever sows generously will also reap generously. Each of you should give what you have decided in your heart to give, not reluctantly or under compulsion, for God loves a cheerful giver. And God is able to bless you abundantly, so that in all things at all times, having all that you need, you will abound in every good work. As it is written: "They have freely scattered their gifts to the poor; their righteousness endures forever." Now he who supplies seed to the sower and bread for food will also supply and increase your store of seed and will enlarge the harvest of your righteousness. You will be enriched in every way so

that you can be generous on every occasion, and
through us your generosity will result in thanksgiving
to God.

—2 Cor. 9:6–11

Tell them to use their money to do good. They should
be rich in good works and generous to those in need,
always being ready to share with others.

—1 Tim. 6:18 NLT

The context of 2 Corinthians 9 is a famine in Jerusalem and Judea. The Jewish world and therefore Jewish Christians were suffering in deep need. The Corinthians had made a promise— an enthusiastic, generous promise to help their Jewish brothers and sisters—and Paul planned to send a delegation to make arrangements to receive their gift.

In the previous chapter, Paul described a very generous church in Macedonia who gave out of their poverty. Generosity doesn't revolve around money as much as getting a new heart and attitude. Paul never taught to give from duty, but from devotion.

The most generous act I have experienced came from an older lady who lived in the middle of a rubber tree plantation in northern Cambodia. A friend and I went on an exploratory trip to check out the possibilities of helping a village build a church. We traveled four hours north of Phnom Penh and arrived at the poorest village I had ever seen up to that point. The village had only a few hundred people, but many of them loved the Lord. Sambat Long, a member of the church I was serving, was from the village. His brother, Channy Long, was the pastor of the village church that met inside his mother's home.

One evening we had a meal with Pastor Long in his home. Homes, which were built on stilts, were just large enough to sleep and eat in. The pictures on the walls came from pictures in magazines. We ate rice, vegetables, and meat together. After the meal, a lady approached the home; she was carrying a coconut with a straw in it. She had heard that there was a visiting pastor in the village and wanted to bring a gift.

It's no secret to people who know me that I have a passionate dislike for coconut. I don't like the smell, texture, or taste. When this lady brought a coconut, I was not really excited . . . until I heard her story. The pastor shared that she was one of the poorest in the community and he had no idea how she had paid for the coconut. It was a gift of sacrifice. She really was the widow in the Bible who brought her two coins to the temple. I was humbled to know I was the recipient of such a gift.

On that day, I loved coconut.

The next day, the village celebrated my friend Sambat's birthday. He was the son coming home, and he had brought friends. They all got together and purchased a side of beef. They hung it from a tree and cut pieces for everyone in the village to share, and we celebrated together. We had a church service where I spoke on God's love. Out of their poverty, this group sang worship and praise to God.

I wonder how God receives our sacrificial gifts. I know I didn't need this lady's coconut. I could have purchased coconuts for the whole village. But as I received the gift with joy, I can only imagine our Heavenly Father's pleasure toward her generosity.

You don't have to be wealthy to be generous; you just have to be willing to share what you have. Generosity is an intentional benevolent act of kindness that serves to the benefit of others and reflects the great God we serve.

Reflection

What is your story? Who has been generous to you? What did that do for you? In what ways is God asking you to be generous?

Prayer

Lord, open my eyes to see the needs around me. As you open my heart, I will open my wallet.

THIRTY-NINE

EXPERIENCE GOD THROUGH GENEROSITY, PART 2

The generous will prosper; those who refresh others will themselves be refreshed.

—Prov. 11:25 NLT

Blessed are those who are generous, because they feed the poor.

—Prov. 22:9 NLT

Command those who are rich in this present world not to be arrogant nor to put their hope in wealth, which is so uncertain, but to put their hope in God, who richly provides us with everything for our enjoyment. Command them to do good, to be rich in good deeds, and to be generous and willing to share. In this way they will lay up treasure for themselves as a firm foundation for the coming age, so that they may take hold of the life that is truly life.

—1 Tim. 6:17–19

Never miss an opportunity to be generous. Err on the side of generosity. I heard those statements years ago, and they play over and over in my head. I am so grateful to whoever said them to me.

Generosity is one of my favorite topics to preach on because I can immediately see what an act of giving can do in someone's heart and life. There is a tangible difference in a person's countenance when someone realizes they blessed someone else. Truly it is more blessed to give than to receive (Acts 20:35). Here are a few of my observations of generous people.

Generous people believe in a generous God and live with grateful hearts. They have an acute understanding that they are blessed and respond by giving to bless others. King David prayed, "Wealth and honor come from you; you are the ruler of all things" (1 Chron. 29:12).

Generous people are not always wealthy people. Wealth has very little to do with generosity. My mom had very little earthly wealth. When she passed away in September 2020, we found that she not only tithed to the church but also supported eight missionaries and several charitable organizations on a monthly basis. She also gave gifts to her family when she felt someone needed help. If she had lived 2,000 years ago, she would have been right next to the widow who gave her two small coins in the temple courts. Jesus said she gave "more than all the others" (Luke 21:3).

Generous people need no recognition. They don't need to announce their gift to the world. In fact, Jesus had a problem with people who proudly displayed their gifts.

Generous people are attractive. They don't complain; they inspire. They are generally upbeat and positive. Who doesn't want to be around that kind of person? Churches are the same way. An atmosphere of generosity attracts generous people.

Generous people are willing to give more when a need arises. Sometimes I personally ask someone to give to a specific need. I realize it is over and above their normal generosity, but they have given me permission to ask.

Generous people don't wait for "someday" to be generous. We can start being generous with whatever God has given us today rather than wait to be able to "afford" it. It is not about the amount; it is about the heart.

Generous people end life well. Those who tend to think they got a raw deal in life end up with resentment. But those who live with gratitude die with a deep sense of the amazing grace that surrounded them.

Reflection

What current opportunities do you have to be generous? It might be as simple as making a pie for someone, or it may cost you dearly. Whatever God is asking you to do, act in quick obedience, and see what God can do in you and through you.

Prayer

God, truly you have been good to me, and the possessions I have come from you. Help me share them with a generous heart. Help me never to miss an opportunity to be generous.

THE HOMEGOING OF A
JESUS-FOLLOWER

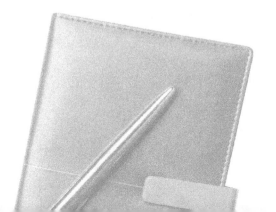

FORTY

EXPERIENCE GOD IN YOUR FINAL BREATH

Precious in the sight of the Lord *is the death of his faithful servants.*

—Ps. 116:15

This seems like a morbid way to end a devotional book, but hang with me for one moment to see that death is truly another reason to be thankful.

In November 2019, my father-in-law, Rudy Kolbe, after weeks of struggling to breathe, took his final lap in the race of life.

In September 2020, my mom drew her final breath. Just two days earlier she said, "Tomorrow, I will be in heaven." She longed to be with her Lord Jesus.

In October 2020, on a Sunday morning, Esther's mom got up, ate breakfast, made her bed, dressed for church, and laid down on her bed to wait for her ride to church. She never woke up. She died exactly how she wanted to.

Within the span of 13 months, my children lost all their grandparents. For all their growing up years, they'd had a front-row seat to watch what it means to live a godly life, to be generous to all, to love missions, to work hard, to support the local church and pastors, to love God's Word, and to remember that this earth is not our home. We celebrate their lives.

The word *precious* means "of great value or high price, like a precious jewel; highly esteemed or cherished, like a precious friend." The Lord values the death of a saint, and God feels our pain over loss. Death does not escape his attention.

Death is our last experience with God on this side of eternity. For some, it comes more quickly than others, but those who have a relationship with Jesus have no need to fear. As the psalmist wrote, "Even though I walk through the valley of the shadow of death, I will fear no evil, for you are with me; your rod and your staff, they comfort me" (Ps. 23:4 ESV).

I drove up to the house of another dear saint in her last days. I thought, "This is her final ascent into God's presence." While standing at her bedside, I read Psalm 121. Her face lit up with a smile as she quoted the chapter with me. To her, these were not simply chapters to read; they were words to live by.

Psalm 121 is one of the "Songs of Ascent," or traveling songs. It was written for God's people as they traveled through rough country terrain to Jerusalem to worship and as they walked up the steps of the temple. They quoted psalms such as Psalm 121 as a means of encouragement. The psalm begins, "I lift up my eyes to the mountains— where does my help come from? My help comes from the LORD, the Maker of heaven and earth" (Ps. 121:1–2). The next two verses say, "He will not let your foot slip—he who watches over you will not slumber; indeed, he who watches over Israel will neither slumber nor sleep" (Ps. 121:3–4).

God knows our every step. He knows our pain, sorrow, joy, and gladness. Our journey is not a matter of indifference to God. He knew the moment we received the news from the doctor that indicated our journey was near completion. He never lost sight of us, and his love never ceased.

Over the years, I have preached more funerals than I care to count, and I can tell you without reservation that people with a personal relationship with Jesus witness God's faithfulness even in their last breath. I have also sat with families who had no belief in God or heaven, and they had no hope, only loss. People who know their loved one is in heaven have an eternal hope that resides within them.

Reflection

Take a moment to let the words of this hymn, written by Fanny Crosby, speak to your spirit.

My Savior First of All

When my lifework is ended and I cross the swelling tide,
When the bright and glorious morning I shall see;
I shall know my Redeemer when I reach the other side,
And His smile will be the first to welcome me.

Chorus:
I shall know Him, (I shall know Him,) I shall know Him,
And redeemed by His side I shall stand;
I shall know Him, (I shall know Him,) I shall know Him
By the print of the nails in His hand.

Oh, the soul thrilling rapture when I view His blessed face,
And the luster of His kindly beaming eye;

How my full heart will praise Him for the mercy, love and grace
That prepared for me a mansion in the sky.

Oh, the dear ones in glory, how they beckon me to come,
And our parting at the river I recall;
To the sweet vales of Eden they will sing my welcome home;
But I long to meet my Savior first of all.

Thro' the gates to the city in a robe of spotless white,
He will lead me where no tears will ever fall;
In the glad song of ages I shall mingle with delight;
But I long to meet my Savior first of all.[21]

Prayer

Jesus, thank you for your comfort, even when it comes time for me to take my final breath or when my loved one goes before me. Thank you for the assurance that to be absent from this body is to be present with you.

---

21. Fanny Crosby, "My Savior First of All," *Hymnary.org*, https://hymnary .org/text/when_my_lifework_is_ended_and_i_cross.

CONCLUSION

Jesus came to seek and to save lost people of whom I certainly qualify. My prayer is for you to experience being found and, in being found, realize the amazing grace of God and live in such a way that sharing God's grace with others becomes a joy.

May the favor of the Lord our God rest on us; establish the works of our hands for us.

—Ps. 90:17

ABOUT THE AUTHOR

Dr. Keith Garfield Edwards is passionate about helping people grow in the grace and knowledge of Jesus Christ. He is the lead pastor of Centerpointe Church in Fairfax, Virginia, and for more than 33 years has served in a variety of ministry positions, including lead pastor, church leadership coach, church planting director, university professor, and missions director. He holds a doctor of ministry from Regent University, a master's degree in pastoral counseling from the Assemblies of God Theological Seminary, and a bachelor of science degree from the University of Valley Forge. He has traveled to more than 25 countries to preach, teach, build, and support the work of missions. Keith and his wife, Esther, have four daughters, two sons-in-law, and two grandchildren—all of whom claim to be the "favorite."